Bloom Where Planted

A True Story by

Winifred Grace and Ava McCarthy

Bloom Where Planted
A true story.

Copyright © 2018 by Winifred Grace & Ava McCarthy

All rights reserved. No part of this book may be reproduced, scanned or distributed in any printed or electronic form without permission.

This is a true story about the life of Ava McCarthy. It is recalled by Ava McCarthy and written by Winifred Grace. All of the names in this book have been changed to protect the privacy of individuals.

10% of all proceeds of this book will be donated to the Deaconess Home in the care of Mr. Gordon; to be used at his discretion because of his limitless love and unwavering devotion to the possibility of change.

Cover Photo Copyright © 2018 by Toni Dota
All rights reserved.

ISBN: 9781724103253

Table of Contents

Author's Note 1

Preface 3

Introduction 11

A Poem - Years Pass 30

Chapter 1 – The Cycle 32

Short Story 61

Chapter 2 – Group Home 67

Chapter 3 – Almost Eighteen 118

Chapter 4 – The Dance 125

Chapter 5 - Tommy 146

A Poem - Tattoos 170

Chapter 6 – Body Modification 172

Chapter 7 – The Turning Point 197

Epilogue 232

Author's Note

It took a year to write this book. I interviewed Ava twice a week, spent the other days researching, transcribing, writing, and editing. The chapters, as they were finished, were returned to Ava and she made changes and returned them to me for more editing, and then repeated again. It was hard for both of us. Difficult for Ava to dig up these memories and difficult for me because they were so hard to hear. I had to be completely numb when I interviewed her in order to move forward, but as I transcribed my notes, tears just fell onto my computer. So much wrong in one life.

This book is true, limited only by Ava's memory. The preface is written by both of us and the introduction is an interview of Ava and members of her family, written in my words and from my perspective about her life. I wrote the chapters in first person from multiple interviews with Ava recounting the memories of her life.

We have changed all of the names, including our own, in order to protect her daughter, my granddaughter, from any "middle school backlash" that so often happens in that age group.

I feel that God inspired, requested, and directed this book and it is done.

Winifred Grace

Preface

Ava McCarthy

As a child in foster care, my imagination would take me to another place and often transport me to another world. I would make up a life that was any life but my own. When I lived with a family that studied Catholicism, I became Catholic. When I lived with a family that didn't have any money, I became a poor girl. Every home presented a new opportunity to reinvent myself and to wear a "different hat." Anything would be better than dealing with my own reality. Hate, anger, and abuse filled my world. The kind of abuse that most people don't want to imagine.

This book is for anyone who will take the time to see life through the eyes of an abused child. I encourage anyone who reads it to see all people as though they were an open book, waiting to be read. Some stories have a fairy godmother and some stories have an evil stepmother. Fairy tales don't always end well. My story did.

I want people who read this book to see how some children live while "in the system." This does not apply to all children in foster care but in my experience, many of us do not know "normal." Normal is a life for kids in "normal" homes with "normal" families. The life I dreamed of having.

I also want all reading this book who find themselves in a similar situation to know that YOU ARE NOT ALONE. Whether you are the abused or the abuser, there is hope. The horrendous cycle can end. There is, and always will be, another way out. Life is about choices, and it is never too late to change your direction.

There are some religious aspects to this book. I am Christian and God has played a big part in my life. Winifred is also Christian, so her views will reflect her beliefs. Although I didn't know it when I was growing up, I think back now and see the different choices I could have made in different situations; choices that He guided me through. My beliefs are my own and they play a big part in my ongoing journey. That being said, you do not need to believe in a higher power in order to read this book.

I hope that this book does not invoke pity but rather courage and inspiration. Imagining life through someone else's eyes, if only temporarily, might forever change your views. My wish is that you, as the reader, act more kindly towards people who are different from you. We all walk different paths and you cannot judge this book by its cover.

Winifred Grace

When I first met Ava I thought my daughter, Annie, had gone mad. Only three years earlier, my daughter had informed me that she was gay. She did this by making a notebook filled with direct quotes from the New Testament that talked of love, acceptance, forgiveness, understanding, and peace. She had suffered in silent hell because of my personal definition of what good, God-fearing "Christians" know to be the truth. That is, you may have feelings about the same sex, but never, ever act upon those feelings. Trying to get the courage to tell a mother like me that you are Christian and you are gay is not easy. It took her years to get the courage to come forward. For this I am ashamed. But that wasn't all.

Up until my daughter met Ava, she had chosen companions who were God-fearing, society-contributing "normal" women. So my narrow-minded thoughts were, "It's okay to have a gay daughter as long as she is dating acceptable women." And then she started dating Ava. It took her awhile to introduce me to Ava; a pole-dancing, tattoo-covered mom who, oh by the way, did not have custody of her child. None of these things were acceptable to me at the time.

Now, I digress for a minute to say something about my daughter's innate value system to always, always do the right thing. For example: when my daughter was in kindergarten and that one little kid on the bus shared that there was no tooth fairy, Annie came home to ask me if that was true. I always knew that when it came time for my children to ask the truth about urban myth, I would tell them the honest truth. So I told my firstborn that, in fact, there was no tooth fairy.

Within minutes, the myth, the man, and the legend known formally as the Easter bunny, as well as the fat man in the red suit, fell apart, as did my Annie. Sitting on the bottom step of the stoop of our home, brokenhearted and crying with her hands over her eyes, rocking back and forth trying to comfort herself, she bellowed out in anguish, "All the parents in all the world are lying to all the children." Annie, from the start of her life, believed in honest goodness.

So when my daughter finally introduced me to Ava, I had been properly prepped that she had some tattoos. I did my best interpretation of acceptance and was cordial but aloof, thinking the entire time, "What does my daughter see in this person? My daughter must want to fix her somehow. Certainly, that has to be the reason."

At this time in my life, I was working full-time, raising kids as a single mom, and attending night classes toward a doctorate. I spent two years writing a dissertation focusing on change, specifically how adults change and then sustain that change. In hindsight, rather than bury myself in research, I should have taken the time to look into a mirror and study my own avoidance. Ironically, I was blind to the fact that I was the one who needed to change.

I was wrong to judge someone based on outward appearance and because of my inability to see without judging, I found out secondhand when Ava and my daughter became engaged in front of friends, with no family present. I, like so many, judged with a human eye and not with the loving grace that God, by His son's example, intended.

This book is about human acceptance of all people at the place where they are in their ever-evolving journey, and more importantly, where they are headed. My hope is that this book softens you, the reader, to begin to view people from the inside and not the outside.

I am honored to be a part of sharing Ava's beautiful story of God's total acceptance and unconditional love, even when you don't know that He is there.

Introduction

This book is not for the faint of heart. This book is about Ava's journey through life thus far. A life that was hard indeed, but is now changed: a cycle that has been broken. Some sections of this book may seem disjointed and even without feeling. It reminds me of Dragnet when the detectives say, "Just the facts, ma'am." This may be because of how hard it is to dig up the past, and the fear of reliving some of the harmful experiences discussed here. It may be because Ava emotionally shut down in order to survive the first part of her life. Maybe there is a void of feeling because she tried not to feel. It may be all of these things.

When talking about generational abuse there needs to be a past generation to speak of. The abuse didn't start with Ava, it ended with her. The generations past go back to her great-great-grandparents. The abuse did not begin there, but that's as far back as we can gather information.

Ava's mother's great-grandfather was abusive. He was an alcoholic with a militant disciplinary style. A deadly combination. He had thirteen children living under one extremely small roof. They could use one square sheet of toilet paper when they went to the bathroom. During his drunk rages, he would get physically abusive with the boys and sexually abusive with the girls. This continued for years until the children moved out of the house and played follow the leader. The children had children and passed down the violence and the shame.

When we interviewed Ava's grandmother, mother, half-sister, and half-brother, they did not share many of the details of their lives and some details they asked that we not share. Together, Ava and I decided that the background information included in this introduction is a necessary piece to explain the puzzle of Ava's life. As horrific as her upbringing was, Ava put it best when she said, "If you are forced to grow up in an abusive home, you don't know 'normal' because that is your 'normal'."

Ava's maternal grandmother refuses to speak about her birth father except to say that "He was a jerk. No fricking good." She has shared stories of sexual abuse with Ava that we have chosen not to publish in this book. She did say to us, "My father was an abuser in a lot of ways. It is probably why I got married so young. Just to get out of the house."

Ava's grandmother began working in a chocolate factory when she was just 15. She met her future husband at the factory. Her brothers introduced them and it was not a fairy tale. She told Ava, "It was not love at first sight. We just hung out." Ava's grandmother and her first husband got married six months after they met. She was 16 and he was 27. She later shared, "I had to get out of the situation I was in (at home) and I walked right into another one."

They had one child together, Ava's mom, Tonya. Things went bad after about two years. "He drank, didn't work, and ran around with his friends." He was not abusive. He just drank all of the time. They were married for five years, and according to Ava's grandmother, "Then I had enough."

Ava's grandmother was in her next relationship for 15 years. She met Grandpa Brown through her mother and his mother. He did a lot of drugs and sold them as well. He was in a well-known biker club and was also a long-haul truck driver with a reputation for impregnating women up and down the East Coast. He had no respect for women or men. What he did to his children did not shock or surprise Ava's grandmother. She just fell in line, happy to have a roof over her head and food in her kids' mouths. According to Ava's grandmother, "I didn't agree with him but I couldn't stop him." She had three boys with Grandpa Brown. Their relationship was tenuous and during an "off" period she got pregnant and had another daughter with a man in the armed forces. She had five children altogether.

Unfortunately, the children raised in this family continued with a cycle of abusive behavior, to themselves and to others. Whenever there was disagreement between the boys in the family, they were told to go outside and "fight like men" until they could resolve their issue. This physical abuse was not limited to the children fighting amongst themselves.

Ava's one uncle recalls a time that his brother did something to anger their father and he "beat his ass with a leather belt so badly that his asshole bled." This same uncle also disclosed information about his dad being so abusive, he would do drugs and get high to escape the torment at home. When his father caught him, he lectured him on his drug use (while he himself was using) and then proceeded to beat him senseless.

One of the boys was killed when he was a teenager while delivering newspapers. The other boys were eventually sent to foster care. When Ava asked her uncle why he was sent away, he could not remember but he referred to the places they were sent as "boys' homes." He would later grow up and end the violent abuse towards his own children, but he was breaking the law a great deal of the time. He has a very long rap sheet and joined the same biker club as his dad. He told Ava stories about the biker club; in order to get in, he had to be tied to a pole for hours and sodomized, molested, and beaten by the "biker bitches." His involvement with this biker club would get him in a lot of trouble and he would do long stints in prison. He recalled a story where he was stripped naked while a group of inmates attempted to rape him. They did not succeed and he hurt them so badly that he ended up in solitary confinement for a year. He shared with Ava that he is ashamed of some of his decisions but has learned a great deal from his past. He has been clean five years now and is educating men in prison on how they can change their lives.

Ava's second uncle has had similar experiences. Unfortunately, this uncle took a different route in life. His first sexual partner was his half-sister. His expression of maladjustment because of his misguided upbringing resulted in the sexual abuse of others and he has served many years in prison.

Ava recalls a time when her mom had gone to work and her uncle came over and started drinking and laughing with the 16-year-old babysitter. She recalls being sent to bed early, but could hear them laughing.

As Ava lay in bed, she heard whimpering and strange noises coming from the couch in the same room. She didn't dare open her eyes. After the noises ended, Ava heard crying, her uncle left, and the babysitter got on the phone. A short time after that, there were cops at the door. Ava remembers that they took her and her half-sister away that night. Ava assumes that this was not the first or last time this happened. Her uncle has been arrested numerous times for exposing himself to small children.

Ava adds, "Growing up, I looked up to my uncles because they were always there to save me from the evils that my mother exposed us to, all the while they themselves were the evil. Looking back, I feel grateful that my sister and I were not part of whatever twisted thoughts they had."

Ava's aunt was not exempt from maladjusted behavior. Although Ava does not know much about her aunt, she had heard stories of drugs and multiple sexual partners. Her aunt met her now-husband and she has gained control over her behavior. As far as Ava is aware, she has never abused her own children, but rather sheltered them from all of her family. She chooses to pretend that her abuse never happened and that her family no longer exists. She literally created a fantasy world for her children to live in, protected from any of their mother's past experiences.

After fifteen years, the marriage between Grandpa Brown and Ava's grandmother dissolved and it would be another two years before Ava's grandmother would meet Grandpa Jack. The only memories Ava's grandmother had with him were good ones. She was a housecleaner and he was a bartender. They traveled together and Ava's grandmother shared that "He was the love of my life." According to Ava's grandmother, their relationship became destructive when his daughter was shot and killed. They separated shortly after.

Tonya, Ava's mother and her grandmother's first daughter, had a similar history as her siblings. Tonya lost her virginity at age ten to her cousin's son. The earliest memories that her mom has are of her stepdad sitting in a big chair and her sitting on a stool in front of him. Even as a young girl she had migraines and he would put a pillow on his lap and massage her head. Later in life, Tonya had brain surgery for aneurysms, but at the time, she was just grateful for some relief. She was completely unaware that he was grooming her for his own agenda. When she was 16 years old, her stepfather raped her and then promised her the world. The sexual abuse escalated to include his friends. When Ava asked her mom if she told anyone, Ava's mom said she told her own mom, but nothing changed and the abuse continued for years.

Tonya became pregnant by her boyfriend and had a son. Her stepfather punched her boyfriend in the face. He left and never came back.

When Tonya turned 18, she married a man named Mitch Malone. They had a son a year later. Tonya shared that she and Mitch went on a late honeymoon to Disney. During this trip, Tonya left her two sons with the neighbors. Oddly, her stepfather paid for the honeymoon and went on the trip with them. When they came back, both of the boys had been severely beaten, with fractured arms and legs and pinholes in their genitals. The oldest son had to be in an incubator for a time after that beating. Since Tonya was not able to prove that she wasn't responsible for the abuse, her boys were put into foster care for four years.

Her first husband ended up going to jail and Tonya did the best she could to survive. While her boys were in foster care, Tonya got pregnant and Ava was born on April 15, in Massachusetts. Two years later Ava's sister Trisha was born to a different father.

As you will discover in this book, much of Trisha's life is intertwined with Ava's. Trisha, Ava's half-sister was abused: verbally, physically, and sexually. She smoked marijuana and was addicted to crack cocaine and methamphetamine (crystal meth) for many years of her life. Trisha had her first child, a girl, when she was 19 years old. She went on to have a boy at 20, a second boy at 22, a second girl at 24, and a third girl at 26 years old. Trisha does not have custody of any of her children. As we write this book, Trisha was just released from a halfway home after spending time in jail. Tonya, Ava's mom, has custody of Trisha's youngest daughter. When we talked to Trisha, she had hope in her voice and was seeing a counselor regularly.

> Sooner or later, I have to deal with my past. Meth made me forget everything that I had bottled up. I'm just so glad I am getting better. It takes a lot of strength to turn your life around and it's not easy. I know it's gonna be hard at times but if you want to get somewhere, you have to work at it. I sorta switched my drug habit. Instead of doing drugs to

pass time, I started working to pass time. (Trisha's conversation with Ava, 10-11-17)

Ava's oldest half-brother, has been in jail but is out on probation, is married, has a job, and is doing well. He has two children and has joint custody of one of them.

Ava's youngest half-brother, was not able to recover from his upbringing as well as his siblings. He is serving a life sentence for the murder of his seven-week-old daughter.

The lives of these people were riddled with abuse, neglect, intolerance, unacceptance, and avoidance. In their world, verbal, sexual, and physical abuse were not uncommon. The avoidance of ever discussing these horrible travesties only led to dark and silent acceptance of truths that they were forced to cover up with lies and deceit.

The havoc that abuse causes for generations cannot be denied. It is handed down like a twisted artifact with no regard for the devastation that it imparts on the unsuspecting recipient. The inheritance handed down in abusive families is shame: never discussed, never recognized, never acknowledged.

Ava's story is a continuation of the abuse that her family passed down from generation to generation with one exception: the heredity of dysfunction has stopped with Ava. Her daughter is living proof of a better way of life. Through the dark past and into the present light, Ava has chosen to stop the cycle and give her daughter a life free from the fear of abuse. Ava's journey through this struggle is painstakingly chronicled in this book.

Many of the horrible travesties she underwent as a child resurfaced while we worked together. Much of the buried past was slowly resurrected during this process. She has the love of God, her partner, her daughter, her family, and the support of a highly competent counselor. Little by little, and ever so slowly, her journey was realized and in the process, healing and self-acceptance were a beautiful byproduct of the truth. The following chapters are recalled by Ava, written by Winifred, and they illustrate Ava's life-journey. The two poems and the short story were written by Ava.

A Poem-Years Pass: Ava writes and shares a poem as a reflection of her early life.

Chapter 1 – The Cycle is an account of life stories that Ava remembers from her past. This chapter recounts Ava's life from birth to age 10 when, after being removed from her home for various reasons and placed into multiple foster homes, she was eventually taken to a psychiatric ward and then transferred to the first of many group homes.

Short Story: Ava shares a short story that she wrote for a college course which recounts the episode that transpired between her and her stepfather as described in Chapter 2.

Chapter 2 – Group Home recounts Ava's life in group homes and in lock-down facilities. Her life from 11 until almost 18 is chronicled in this chapter. It was a time of rebellion against any person or agency that tried to control her.

Chapter 3 – Almost 18 is a dark and graphic description of sexual abuse at the hands of a stranger. It is the culminating event of so many prior injustices that led to an early life of indifference to her own treatment and her indifferent treatment of others.

Chapter 4 – The Dance gives vivid details of the kind of turmoil that is so often the result of repeated abuse. Ava shares her experiences as a dancer in multiple night clubs and the perils that resulted from this lifestyle.

Chapter 5 – Tommy recounts the time that Ava spent with the father of her daughter. It was a time of perceived security for Ava but the dysfunction caused by addiction makes this story sad and short-lived.

A Poem – Tattoos: Ava writes and shares her feelings regarding her tattoos.

Chapter 6 – Body Modification gives the reader a look into Ava's young adult life. She searched for a relationship in every partner she encountered but had no idea what constituted a healthy relationship. Her partners were many and the tattoos that she obtained during this time were many as well. Some had meaning and some were just to pass the time, both the partners and the tattoos.

Chapter 7 – The Turning Point shares a vision of change and hope. It is Ava's journey from out of the dark, into the light. This chapter is written from the perspective of Ava and her partner. Through their honest account of growth and change, Ava's story thus far is brought to fruition.

The Epilogue contains Ava's closing thoughts.

A Poem - Years Pass

Leaving the security of the insulated womb

Pushed into a brightly lit room by hands covered in latex

A stranger gently handing a new life

Passed off to a woman, a stranger, into her arms I go

Feeling her heart beat pounding beneath her warm skin

Time passes

Leaving all sense of security behind I leave a path

Of broken hopes and false promises.

A stranger has arrived to take me away

Into the arms of this person unknown

Forced to live with strangers

Insecure and alone

Being told to trust in the system

Believe what they say

Years pass.

Another trail of destruction and despair

No hope for a better tomorrow

Only living for today

What stranger's arms will hold me tonight
Empty emotions continue to fill this hollow heart
Years pass
This trail has become a deep routed path
Strangers become strange
Feelings become distorted
A façade
An illusion of the mind

Chapter 1 – The Cycle

I don't know who my dad is. I have a strong suspicion that my birth-father is my step-grandpa, Grandpa Brown. My mother, Tonya does not consider this a possibility but I can't help but wonder. It just always seemed strange to me that he paid for and went on her honeymoon with her. Why would he if the abuse was not continuing? I always thought I looked like my step-grandfather and I have his mannerisms. I was never permitted to play at his house alone or be around him. My mother was not one to instill rules, but that rule she kept.

At three weeks old I was removed from the home. Tonya said she did not know who called children's services or why. She said, "There was a crib and a walker and I had everything I needed." According to the reports, there was no heat or electricity in the building, so I was placed into foster care until I was nine months old. When Tonya went before the judge, she said that she was told that she could only keep one child. She opted to keep me because "the boys were already together and she wanted them to stay together." My half-brothers were later adopted.

Nine Months to Four Years

When I was nine months old, Tonya was living with her boyfriend Matt. A few months after I was allowed to return to my mom's home, Matt and Tonya had a daughter, my half-sister Elizabeth. I think Matt was a good man and he had my name and Elizabeth's tattooed on his arm. He thought of me as his daughter. Unfortunately, their life was not calm.

Bloom Where Planted

One night, when Elizabeth and I were sleeping and Tonya was playing cards, two women knocked at the apartment door and asked for Matt. Apparently, a front for Tonya's ex-husband who was just released from jail and coming for Matt, they chased Tonya and pulled her ponytail hard enough to throw her down. She was bleeding and kicking and fighting the two girls off, and finally sirens could be heard and the women ran away.

Very soon after that incident, at three weeks and two days old, my half-sister Elizabeth died of Sudden Infant Death Syndrome. My mom said Matt couldn't deal with her death and he left us. Matt shared a different story. He said that Tonya cheated on him and then he went to jail so they split up.

Tonya remembers moving to Georgia shortly thereafter and meeting a man named Travis. She worked at a truck-stop diner and he worked at a roadside fruit stand. They had my half-sister Trisha in 1987. Tonya and Travis decided to leave Georgia and move to Tampa, Florida. Travis made a living selling tomatoes out of a station wagon. The money was not enough and life quickly took a turn for the worse. As money got tighter, Travis became progressively more abusive until Tonya was afraid for her life and she turned to the neighbors for help. They took us to the airport and paid for the trip. With only the clothes on our backs, Tonya, Trisha, and I left for Massachusetts.

According to Tonya, Travis was so angry about her leaving with his daughter that he followed us to Cape Cod and tried to kidnap Trisha. The police escorted him to the border of the state and Tonya never saw him again.

Four Years to Six Years

When I was young, my best friend's name was Stephanie and I thought she was rich. She lived across the street and had all the "New Kids on the Block" music and all of the doll figures that represented the singers. She had curtains in her windows and sheets on her bed.

We would spend hours down at a nearby dock carefully pulling jellyfish out of the water, then putting them on the ground to watch them disappear. We would go into the nearby woods that hid a secret blanket of lady slippers, and we would pick bouquets of pink and purple treasures for ourselves. With long stems and leaves, they were just so consistent in their appearance. The sweet smell was like an escape to a perfect hideaway in the woods. We loved popping snapdragons, opening their mouths to talk to the other flowers about important young girl topics. Stephanie later moved to Florida and I never saw her again, but these are my best childhood memories.

While in Massachusetts, Tonya found work around race cars. She sold glow sticks and other trinkets at the track. It was at the race track that she met her boyfriend, Charlie. Some of my first memories as a child were very loud noises coming from Tonya's bedroom. I now know that she and Charlie were having sex, but when I was little, they were just making loud knocks on the walls, screams, and breathing noises. Stephanie and I would go into my room and laugh and make fun of their noises.

Charlie was a bad man. When Tonya was at the track, he would lock me in the bathroom or in the basement for hours on end. I remember just screaming and screaming. If my screams got to be too much for Charlie, he would put a pillow over my face until I passed out. I tried to tell my mom but she called me "dramatic." I learned not to scream. This later manifested itself as severe claustrophobia and when I was in foster care, they would have to check that there was no bathroom light switch outside the door in order for me to be in that home. I had terrible panic attacks if I thought someone could lock me in any room with the lights off.

Charlie would pull down my pants and slap me with a leather belt if I didn't eat what I was told. I remember waking up in the mornings sometimes to bruises all down my back. I didn't know why. When I showed Tonya she would say, "Maybe you slept weird." While my lack of sleep may have been one problem, the bigger issue at hand was my attendance at school. I missed 135 days in first grade.

I was six when Trisha and I were removed from Tonya's house again. Trisha had run around in the neighborhood naked and one of the neighbors called the police. When the police arrived, they brought the social workers. I remember a police officer telling her, "You need to surrender the kids to DSS" (Department of Social Services). Tonya just kept repeating, "What? I don't understand" over and over and over.

The police had already taken Trisha to the car, but I knew better. I was not leaving with any social worker because I knew that social workers would take me away from my mom. I screamed that I was not leaving with a social worker.

One of the police officers said I could ride in the car with him. I believed him but when I got outside of the door, the social worker grabbed me and took me away. All I could do was scream. I never trusted a caseworker after that day. It was the first time I truly remember becoming a ward of the state.

The Cape with Bob and Lydia, Six to Seven Years

Foster care with Bob and Lydia seemed crowded. Trisha and I were six and four and they had two children. Lydia was extremely overweight and baked cakes for a living. Bob was overweight as well and smelled like an old garage and cheap cologne.

We lived on a dead-end road and often played outside. There were some fun memories at the Cape.

Kick the Can, and Man Hunt (a more intense game of tag with flashlights) were regular events with all the kids. I remember running until my legs just burned and I had to stop, bend over, and catch my breath. But there always seemed to be more wrong than right.

My first exposure to a lesbian experience was on the Cape. We had a babysitter one night and we were outside playing Man Hunt. The babysitter kept screaming at us to go outside and "fuck off." She had a friend over and I remember thinking, "Something is going on and I want to find out what." So I crawled on my belly into Bob and Lydia's bedroom, poked my head under the bed sheets, and saw our babysitter and her friend naked. I just thought that was so strange and I ran out to tell everyone, "There are two naked girls inside that bed." I didn't know if it was wrong or if it was hilarious, but I know I was intrigued by the fact that they were two girls together. I never told any adults but I'm sure one of the other kids told on them because we never saw that babysitter again.

I remember one time we were playing Nintendo downstairs and Trisha was upstairs playing Hide and Seek with the boys. She came down all bloody and had to get stitches in the back of her head. But that wasn't the worst of the Cape.

Bob liked us girls to sit on his lap and would stroke our hair while we watched movies or played video games. He never did this with all of us at the same time, always individually. I thought it was strange that he would only take the girls to the candy store, never any of the boys. He gave all of the girls in the house baths at the same time. At bedtime we were only allowed to wear nightgowns, never pajamas with pants. It was at this foster home I remember being touched inappropriately for the first time.

On Thanksgiving day I was sent to my room for talking back. Going to bed without anything to eat caused me to wake up in the middle of the night, stomach growling. I decided to sneak into the kitchen to get some leftover food. I was as quiet as I could be but was met in the kitchen by Bob. I was anxious and worried he was going to be really mad at me for stealing, but instead, Bob sat me down at the table and made me a plate of food. I ate it so fast I got horrible hiccups. I remember I had on a little nighty with teddy bears and a flimsy little pair of underwear that were too big. I am pretty sure they were hand-me-downs since new clothes were hard to come by at that house.

Bob took me upstairs to tuck me into my bed. His large calloused hands brushed against my small legs. I could hear him breathing heavy and fast. I was so scared because I knew something was wrong. I just couldn't yell or scream. I was too petrified to move. He proceeded to stick his finger inside of me. It hurt me. I could see his other hand making a fast motion, an act that I now know to be masturbation. But then in my teddy bear pajamas, I was just a little girl who was scared and hurting.

The abuse went on for weeks. I began to refuse to bathe. I tried to tell Lydia and then I told my caseworker. They did not believe me. I remember I had to sit in a room for hours and play with a doll. I had to show them where my "no-no" parts were and where I was claiming that I was touched.

Finally, we were removed from their home.

Years later I worked at a bakery and Lydia was the cake decorator. She told me, "I'm sorry that I didn't believe you, Ava. I got divorced from Bob."

Foxborough – Roberta's House, Seven to Eight Years

Roberta was old but was nice. She had adult children and two additional foster children besides Trisha and me. I wanted to be adopted by her. She was always kind to us and made sure that we ate healthy and took us on adventures in her blue minivan. Roberta would take us to scheduled visits with Tonya at the foster care center. Tonya was allowed two visits a week. She only showed up every couple of months but Roberta always got us there for the appointments. She got me a pair of Barbie roller skates that you strapped on your shoes. I had a bike and we were allowed to ride around the cul-de-sac. Although there was a jungle gym in her back yard, the very best thing about Roberta's yard was that she lived behind the Patriots stadium. We would have to stay outside at night until "Golden Girls" was over so we would listen to the games.

It was because of Roberta that I learned about organized religion. Roberta made us go to a Catholic church with her every Sunday. I remember it was boring and my knees hurt. Every so often, they wanted people to eat wafers. Roberta would allow her grandkids to eat the wafers but not us. Maybe because we weren't "real" Catholics. Maybe she thought we were a lost cause. Whatever the reason, I wanted to eat them and we weren't allowed. One time Megan, Roberta's granddaughter, snuck a wafer out for me. Roberta was very angry that I got a wafer, but I was just listening to her yell while trying really hard to get the wafer off the roof of my mouth.

The "real" kids at Roberta's house, her grandkids, were in sports and extra activities and the foster kids were not. It didn't matter to me. I wanted to live there forever. It was at Roberta's house that I began to refer to myself as "Chameleon." I would assume the identity of the grandkids and other foster kids. My foster sister was in a Shirley Temple recital. I memorized all of her lines and told everyone that I was in the recital. I lied compulsively about my past.

Those were not all of the changes I was going through at Roberta's house. Roberta was good but her grandson was not.

Jerry was Roberta's son. He and his wife Jessica had two children, Jerry Jr. and Megan. Trisha and I would go with them to their kids' sporting events. Jerry Jr. was my age. We would camp out in the back yard and he would tell me it was okay to touch his penis. I did not know this was bad or wrong. It escalated to hand jobs, oral sex, and eventually to dry humping. Megan called her brother "Sex Machine" and although we only kissed in front of her, she knew what was happening. I know now that this unhealthy experimentation with sexual acts at this young age was a result of the sexual abuse I experienced at the hand of Bob. But at the time, it just seemed like something I was supposed to do. When Jerry Jr. told me to perform sexual acts with him, I did. I didn't hate it or like it. I just did it. Jerry Jr.'s other grandmother caught us one time but she never said anything to anyone. She told us to stop and walked out of the room.

Even though I wanted to stay with Roberta, time ran out in foster placement and, once again, we went to live with Tonya.

Back Home, Eight Years

Dan was Tonya's second husband. He had shoulder-length black hair and really dark eyes. He had a son, Dan Jr., who would stay with us once in a while. Dan was like a father to us but he was extremely controlling. He would take us bike riding and skating. He was really a good stepdad when he wasn't drinking. Unfortunately, he was rarely sober.

If there was lunch meat, it was only for him, we were never allowed to touch it. If there was milk, it was just for him. I did get around that at times by pouring water in the milk jug after I drank some of it. I would study exactly where the milk line was and exactly where he placed it in the refrigerator. It was like a science. We went to the soup kitchen a lot for our meals. Even when I was little, I was so prideful, I would never eat at that place. I just never felt like I belonged there. People were homeless and smelled and I hated it.

At home, Dan would throw his empty bottles of alcohol outside of the house and there was glass everywhere. We never had shoes and my feet were so calloused that the glass never cut me.

We lived on the second floor. I remember a guy we called "Uncle Joe" who was visiting one time and he hung me out the window by my ankles. He must have thought it was a joke because he was laughing the whole time. My mom walked up the driveway and screamed, "Get my fucking kid inside that window now," and he pulled me back in. Home wasn't what I would call a "good situation," but it was home, and the only one I knew.

We did have a great neighborhood for friends to hang out. Shana Peters (my best friend), Megan (who called herself "Megan the Midget"), the Thompson Twins, and Justine. Shana Peters's mom worked at the Dollar Store so it was easy to steal things there. My mom worked at Dunkin' Donuts and we would steal change from the tip jar and throw the stolen change into the snow. We couldn't always find the change and when the snow melted, we were so excited to find those shiny coins on a blanket of green grass. In the summer, I remember picnics in the park with mayo and mustard sandwiches, all of us kids just hanging out.

Bloom Where Planted

I remember going to the house of my Grandpa Caravelli, my mom's dad, to visit often. He was my favorite person. He was an alcoholic and somewhat of a hoarder but he was a happy drunk and loved to sing. He would pay cab drivers to get his alcohol from the "packie" (anyplace where you buy alcohol) well before Uber had the idea. He made big churches from match sticks and they were beautiful. Grandpa Caravelli just loved life and I loved going over there; I had plenty of time to do so since I rarely went to school.

I do remember when I did go to school and they had fundraisers, I would take orders and collect the money and never turn it in to the school. One time we got ahold of a UNICEF box and went around collecting money for the charity. Shana Peters and I spent the money. We figured we were poor, so it was okay.

Shana Peters and I used to collect cans and take them to the packie because they would recycle them. It didn't take long until we discovered that they put all the cans into big garbage bags around the back. As soon as we found that out, we just stole garbage bags from the back of the store, took the cans out of the bags, and turned them in for money in the front of the store.

There was one guy in the neighborhood named Greg. He might have been in his late teens and we knew to stay away from him because he was bad. We heard rumors about him doing sexual things to little kids. One day Shana Peters and I were changing my bike chain and Greg asked if we wanted to play Doctor. We decided to capture him. We brought him back to our house and we trapped him in the basement. My mom came down and got him out. As he ran away my mom yelled, "Stay the fuck away from my kid." He was punching at the air, stomping, and screaming, but he left us alone after that.

I was at Shana Peters's house when my sister set the house on fire. Trisha was playing with my stepbrother and they found some matches. The curtains caught on fire first and the next thing they knew, the apartment was going up in flames. I came running home and was blamed for the fire, I think because I used to like to set papers on fire in the tub.

Foster Care at Roberta's Son's House, Eight to Nine Years

After the fire, we were placed in Jerry and Jessica's house. I don't know how we ended up being placed in Roberta's son's house. It seems too unlikely that it would just be a coincidence. Jerry's wife Jessica had braces and very curly hair. Jerry was tall and owned a business that brought mail all around the town. I remember that Jerry had a car phone and, at the time, I thought that was really cool. They had a big back yard on a lake. We would play on the shoreline in the warmer months and in the winter we would ice skate. There was a penny candy store not too far from the house, and we would ride our bikes there all the time.

At this time of my life, I actually thought I was a boy. My foster placements kept my hair very short (maybe to avoid lice) and I had no breasts yet. When I first started my period, I would get a white discharge in my underwear and I knew that happened to boys. I didn't know what to do about the discharge so I just kept throwing my underwear out. When the discharge turned darker, I would take toilet paper balls and put them up my vagina to keep the blood from coming out. I did this until I was 12.

My cousins Marissa and April lived on the same road, so I went over to their house almost every day. Probably because things were so bad at Jerry and Jessica's. As soon as we were placed in their foster home, the sexual acts between Jerry Jr. and I immediately started back up. We never had intercourse, but I was too young for sexual activity and I began to act out in any way I could.

I developed a very bad problem of hiding food. I would hide it in the curtains and under the bed, anywhere I could so that I knew where I could find it later. I couldn't help but feel that I might need the food. It was a compulsion that I could not control even when I got into trouble. I just couldn't stop.

It was at this time that I began cutting myself. I remember either Jerry or Jessica had to sit outside of my door while I bathed or went to the restroom for any reason. I began to run away from their house all the time. I assume this became a liability for them as foster parents. It wasn't long before I was removed and sent back home.

Back Home Again, Nine Years

When we went back home, it didn't take long for the bad things to start up again with Dan. Mariska and Deni were two kids in our neighborhood. They were even poorer than we were so we didn't always hang out with them. We thought they were trashy and we knew they were trouble. One night, Mariska slept over and accused my stepfather, Dan, of molesting her. I don't know if it was true or if they were trying just to get back at us for being "fake friends." He got arrested but the charges didn't stick and he got out of jail shortly after.

When Dan got out, things got a lot worse. He was drinking a lot so Tonya was gone every night playing Bingo. I don't remember if it was Easter or the day before Easter but Dan Jr., Trisha, and I were on the living room floor watching Pet Sematary. Dan came home very intoxicated and very angry. Dan Jr. went into the bedroom. He probably didn't want to get hit.

Dan started cracking eggs over my sister's head. He was yelling over and over again that I needed to change my sister's underwear. I don't know why, but he kept saying that she was dirty. After all of the yelling, he picked up Trisha by her hair and threw her; she literally flew in the air. When I asked Trisha about it, she said she remembered him dragging her by her hair. Then she said, "I guess that stuff I just blocked out." Although Trisha was hurting, I got the brunt of it that day.

My sister and I had some glass cups on the floor from coloring Easter eggs. Dan smashed my face into one of the cups and started pounding on me. It seemed like forever, but eventually he stopped. I don't know if he got bored or tired but he went to sleep. Trisha and I cleaned each other up. I have a scar on my lip from him hitting my face into the glass cup.

Not long after this happened, we had a pregnant babysitter at the house. She invited her boyfriend over and when Trisha and I came out of the bedroom, he was performing oral sex on her right at the kitchen table. They kept yelling, "Fuck off" but I wouldn't leave them alone. I wanted them to stop because I didn't want my sister to see them. The verbal obscenities escalated until eventually the boyfriend came after me. I stood up on the counter and started throwing cans of food at them. Then I started throwing steak knives. I took my sister into my mom's room and held a butcher knife to Trisha's neck. I had no intention of hurting her and I told her over and over again, "I'm not gonna hurt you Trishie." I wouldn't hurt her. I just wanted the babysitter to get out of our house. But the cops came. I was scared but it felt like a game. It was cool to have so much attention. I made demands. They didn't respond with any of my requests but I thought it might work.

Finally, I let her go and they rushed in and threw my little nine-year-old body down on the ground and pinned me there. I was scared and alone so I just screamed. But no one was listening. They put me in a police car and took me to a hospital and so my group home experiences began.

Trisha recalls the episode but states, "I knew you weren't going to hurt me." Trish shared with me recently that when I left for the group home, she was so sad. We were separated for the first time and although I'm not sure I was much help; I was the only help she had.

Short Story

"Ava! Get your ass out here now!" The voice screaming from the kitchen was my stepfather.

I came scurrying out of my bedroom where I had been hiding all day with my younger sister.

"Yes?"

"Why do you and your sister think it's o.k. to leave this shit all over the house?"

It was Easter Sunday. My sister and I had been playing with an Easter egg dying kit. We had unfortunately neglected to pick it up.

"I am so sorry." I squealed, my voice cracking. The overwhelming feeling of nausea entered my stomach. My face went pale as I waited for what my punishment would be.

"Damn right you are sorry!"

The beer in his hand was ice cold. I remember seeing the droplets of water hit the floor as his hands waved around frantically. The air in the room suddenly felt suffocating. Focusing on the water droplets put me in a state of serenity.

At the young age of nine, I was often forced to put myself into a trance-like state. My mind would leave my body. Tonight was no different.

His hard, calloused hands formed tight fists. Before I could squirm away, his fist had made contact with my jaw. Blackness all around me. No pain. No feeling. Only the feeling of finally being at peace.

Slowly my eyes stared to flutter open, barely able to see past the dried blood that had begun to build up around my eyes. I just lay there. Not wanting to face my reality just yet.

Bloom Where Planted

I imagined myself as a superhero. My superpower? Well, it would be a conscience. Not my own conscience. Rather that of my stepfather. I would allow myself to creep slowly into his mind. I would wake up in his mind when his eyes opened at the dawns first light. As his feet hit the floor, I would be there waiting to guide him in a different direction. When he went off to work, as he drove home. Especially when he cracked open that first can of bubbling beer. That's when I would make my move. I would whisper into his soul, "You do not need this beer, think about your kids in the other room. It is Easter, be present and in the moment." My soothing tones would make him think twice.

As my failed superpower attempts get me discouraged, I cannot allow myself to believe my powers are not enough to get through to him. His anger levels rise with each beer he guzzles down. Each beer he drinks goes down faster than the last. My kind words and whispers seem to go unnoticed.

As he gets up off the old beat-up couch, he stumbles around trying to regain his balance. Bored with himself, he wanders into my sister's room. Raging about nonsense. As she starts to cry from sheer panic, I yell a silent yell that only he can hear. "STOP!"

He leans all his weight on the rotted door panel, drops his beer and walks away. Crashing in his unmade bed. One leg and arm off the edge as the rest of his overweight body is still. Drooling into his pillow as he starts to sleep off his latest binge.

My eyes are fully open. Pain is coursing through my entire body. I lift my frail arm up to see what damage has been done. Numb. Blood dried up in the corner of my mouth. My little sister is now stroking my mousey brown hair in an attempt to ease my suffering.

Suddenly reality has set in. Fight or flight.

Allowing myself just a few moments to realize what had happened, I slowly start to crawl into the bathroom to clean my face. My once-pale cheeks are now covered in black and blue bruises.

"Ice! I need ice," I cried to my sister. She ran into the kitchen; I was scared of what she would find in there.

Silence. Minutes felt like hours. Our ears were perked for any noise or movement.

Nothing.

We left the entombed bathroom. The lights had been cut off earlier that week. It was quickly getting dark outside. Two hours had passed.

I lit a candle and said a silent prayer.

I found myself walking bravely into my parents' room. There I found my stepfather.

One leg and arm off the edge as the rest of his overweight body lay on the bed. Drooling into his pillow as he started to sleep off his latest binge.

Chapter 2 – Group Home

After the police took me from Tonya's house, they drove me to the hospital for a psychiatric evaluation. The psych ward smelled so badly, I almost got sick to my stomach. The permeating smell of vomit, blood, and excretion covered with a thick layer of Lysol was horrific. I was there for a few days and then was transferred to Arbour-Fuller Hospital in Massachusetts.

Arbour-Fuller Hospital

The staff at Fuller admitted me at night and I was immediately given Trazadone[1] so I would sleep. This process became common during my three weeks in the

---

[1] "Trazodone, sold under the brand name Oleptro among others, is an antidepressant of the serotonin antagonist and reuptake inhibitor (SARI) class. It is a phenylpiperazine compound. Trazodone also has anti-anxiety (anxiolytic) and sleep-inducing (hypnotic) effects. https://en.wikipedia.org/wiki/Trazodone"

psychiatric ward. The next few days were filled with so many questions it made my head spin. "Why did you want to kill your sister?" "What did you hope to gain by confronting the police?" "What were you thinking; then, now, every minute?" I hated it and I had no problem showing it through continuous confrontation with everyone.

I had a roommate in the hospital and she was awful. She had delusions of being a Roman goddess. Quite often, she would wait until I was sleeping at night and try to attack me. I would lock her out of the room all the time in an attempt to have some privacy. The aides would barge in and I would fight them, and they would put me on the bed and strap me down with a six-point restraint.[2] They usually gave me a shot in my rear

---

[2] A six-point restraint involved being restrained face-down while strapping both wrists, both ankles, waist, and head to the bed.

end and I would sleep for a few hours while the medicine took its toll. This became routine the majority of my nights.

After a few weeks of my roommate's nightly episodes, I asked my mother to bring me a teddy bear with a knife hidden inside. She obliged. As I write this it seems strange that my mother would do such a thing. Actually bring a bear with a knife hidden in it to a hospital for a kid! To understand her behavior necessitates understanding mine. I was masterful at manipulation. I could talk my mother into doing almost anything. For instance, on one visit I talked her into piercing my nose. She brought an earring from home, took a carrot off of my dinner tray, put it in my nostril, and pierced my nose in the room.

The very night that my mom brought the bear, I waited for that goddess to jump on me in the dead of night and I held the knife to her throat and told her, "If you come after me again I will slit your throat."

She told on me the next day. When they came for me, I barricaded myself in the room and they had what seemed like all of the staff trying to break into my room. They eventually busted through the door and accused me of "inciting a riot." It took six shots in my ass for them to calm me down after they strapped me in that night. I woke up two days later. My butt was completely black and blue. Later, someone told me that the incident caused a riot on the floor. I never told them that my mother brought the knife in the bear but later they changed the policy in the ward. No more stuffed animals in the units.

Bloom Where Planted

After the bear episode, I was forced to go on my first medication, Zoloft. The routine was Zoloft in the day and Trazodone at night. I felt like a zombie all of the time. The ward had a certain protocol for medication distribution. We were to go to the nurses' station certain times of the day, stand in line, and receive the prescribed pills. We had to lift our tongues to show that we had swallowed the pills. For some reason, I just couldn't follow that routine. To stand in line and willingly take a drug that I hated was not something I could do.

It was not uncommon for me to "freak out" at the nurses' station. I didn't want to do anything they wanted me to do. I would throw the pill at the nurse and the aides would come to restrain me. This usually resulted in me screaming "fuck off" to the aides. Whatever I could do to avoid taking the medicine, I would do. I would hit and kick and spit. These incidents would always end with them carrying me back to my room, strapping me down, and giving me the meds anyway. Somehow, that was better than me giving in to them and losing my control. What they saw as a loss of control in my behavior was actually my only way to fight for control over what went into my body, what went on in my life. I never won the battles, but it didn't matter to me. I just wasn't going to stand in line and take the medication willingly.

One time, I convinced all the girls to cheek[3] their meds, and I hid them in the

---

[3] It was common practice to hide medicine in your cheek rather than swallow the pills. You could sell them, trade them, or save them up if you plan an overdose.

lining of my underwear. Later that night, I tried to overdose on all the meds I had collected. I obviously survived but did find out that I am allergic to Paxil.

Aside from my behavior, the ward was actually set up to run smoothly. A regular day consisted of various times of freedom or confinement depending on conduct. The choices were 50-10, 45-15, and 30-30. The first number referred to how many minutes you spent locked down in your room, the second referred to how many minutes you spent in the community room. If you were following the rules, you got to sit in the community room and watch MTV videos or just "hang out." If you had all of your privileges, you could go to the cafeteria for breakfast, lunch, and dinner as well as an occasional snack. I only got to go to the cafeteria one time because my privileges were revoked on a regular basis. I usually had to stay in the unit and eat, but some of the other girls would bring me their snacks, hot cocoa packets or graham crackers and peanut butter, and I would hide in my room and eat them quietly and by myself.

After a very long three weeks I was released and sent back home.

Home Meeting

My mom was still with my stepfather, Dan, and I was always acting out. I had a habit of pretending to kill myself. Not only would I tell my mom I was going to hurt myself, but I would call her at Dunkin' Donuts, where she worked, and tell her that I had done something to cause her to have to leave work. I have one memory of getting pills out of the cabinet and laying them all around me, all over the floor. Then I just lay down on the kitchen floor waiting for her to come home. Another time I splattered ketchup all over the bathroom and lay on the floor like I'd slit my wrists. I don't remember ever having any intention of killing myself; I just wanted to act it out and get my mom's attention.

I don't know if my mom called the social worker or if the Department of Developmental Services did a routine follow-up at the house, but whatever the reason, I was evaluated. Apparently they were worried about me harming myself so I was taken to my first group home. I was ten years old.

Lancaster Ten to Eleven Years

Lancaster was a large campus with a big building that housed many children. They had horses and it was surrounded by woods. Inside there were long hallways that seemed to never end. There were four kids to a room with two sets of bunkbeds. We did a lot of group activities but I didn't like it there.

My mom would visit me and bring me candy bars and Sprite. To me, it didn't matter what she did to try and make up for one simple fact: she had put me in there and left. So nothing really mattered to me except that I didn't want to be told what to do, and the more they told me what to do, the worse I behaved.

They had timeout rooms. These rooms had padded walls and big metal doors with a rope on the outside of the handle. The staff would close the door and hold it so it was impossible to get out. There was a television monitor so the staff could watch the behavior of anyone in the room, but other than that, no bed and no chair. I was in that timeout room for what seemed like all the time.

I would walk around the room in a circle just screaming and swearing. It didn't take me long to figure out that if I hit my head on the wall until it bled, they had to come in and restrain me. One time, I don't remember what I did, but they had me in that room for the day. I just couldn't calm down so they left me in there. After some time, I had to use the restroom, but they wouldn't take me so I urinated and defecated in the room. When they came to put me in a clean room, they looked like the scientists when they dressed like astronauts in "E.T." I threw my feces at those people. I learned that trick from another girl in the home. I started urinating in my clothes when they put me in timeout and when the staff would come in and say my time was up, I would throw my wet underwear at them. It was fun for me to see them duck. One time I hit one staff worker's face and she swore at me. I heard later that she got in trouble for that. I just thought it was funny.

I studied the behavior of other girls in the home. One other girl loved to eat anything. She would eat pieces of wood that she found on the floor or literally anything she found. One time she ate a screw.

I don't remember the name of the girl with whom I ran away the first time. A boy named Corey distracted the staff while we snuck out the back door. The woods were so dense we could hardly see in front of us. We ran as fast as our young legs would allow. Someone must have snitched on us because we weren't even out of the woods when we heard the staff calling us. We knew that they were hot on our trail.

Bloom Where Planted

The woods were thick but the mosquitoes were thicker. I felt as though I was bitten on every part of my exposed skin. After what seemed like an eternity, we found a yard and hid under a porch. The staff were right outside when a dog came up to the porch and started sniffing around. For some reason, they didn't notice the dog and the first chance we had, we ran again and wound up in someone's shed. In the shed, we found a big bottle of unmarked liquid. We decided together that if the police found us we would throw it into their faces.

The mosquitoes persuaded us to go ask the homeowner if we could stay with her. At the time, it seemed like a good idea until we found out that the lady who lived in the house had a daughter who worked at the group home we had just run from. She gave us milk and cookies and told us everything was going to be fine. She called the police from another room.

The police came in the house, but no one was listening when the girl and I talked about drinking the liquid in the unmarked bottle, which I later learned was antifreeze. The other girl and myself were freaking out; as she started to "drink" the unmarked liquid, I panicked. I asked her repeatedly if she had drunk it and she said, "Yes." I did not know that she was lying when I began to chug the liquid.

Immediately my throat was on fire. It was so cold, it was hot, and I went into a seizure. The adults thought I was just acting so they just held me down. When the ambulance came, I remember the paramedics being mad and yelling that I had drunk something. There was a lot of panic all around me. Two bottles of

Ipecac and a great deal of water later, I must have gone unconscious because the hurting stopped.

I woke up in the hospital and I was temporarily blind. I was barely 11 and I was so scared by myself in that hospital bed. For three days I lay there unable to see. When I did regain my sight, the doctor told me I would be legally blind by the age of 27. I went from 20/20 vision to needing very strong glasses for the rest of my life. I was in the hospital for the remainder of the week, and then I went back to the psychiatric ward for a while. It was more of the same behavior; I acted out, they strapped me down, and I was medicated. I constantly battled the ghosts of my past that haunted me but were invisible to anyone around me.

Natick Group Home, Eleven to Twelve Years

My next home looked like a group of different houses on one big property. There were multiple rooms in each house and five girls to a room. The first two weeks I was there, I refused to eat. When I finally was tempted, it was with peanut butter and marshmallow Fluff.

There were constant group meetings but I thought they were a waste of my time. At this home, they took the shoes for 10 days from people who tried to run away. I tried to run away the very first day and several times after that. I had my shoes the first day and the last day for my year-long stay at Natick.

I was the youngest girl by far at this home so I learned a great deal from the older girls. I learned about sex, even though I really didn't know what that was yet. The older girls told me on a regular basis that I was a boy. I was very small, skinny, and flat-chested. I had gotten my first period when I was nine but I did not know what a period was. It wasn't until I was 12 that a girl walked in on me in the bathroom stall as I was rolling up toilet paper and putting it up my vagina. She screamed at me, "What the fuck are you doing?" and I told her. She told me it was a period, gave me a tampon, and showed me how to use it.

When I had the opportunity, it seemed like a good idea to shave my head with a Bic razor, leaving just bangs. Edwin, a boy from the other unit, liked me and would write me love letters, fold them into a football, and flick them at me. He told me he liked my shaved head.

The older girls were instrumental in promoting the many times I ran away. They probably thought it was funny to see me repeatedly try to run. I just liked the attention. They were always helping me come up with a new plan. One time I ran and got through the woods to an exterior chain-link fence. I tried to jump the fence but my jeans got caught on the pointed metal at the top. My pants ripped from the crotch to the bottom leg. I was literally hanging there. While pulling myself up, I hooked my other pant leg and it did the same thing. I finally got free and both pant legs were split from the top to the bottom. It did not stop me from running.

The policeman who found me later said I was lucky he got to me because I was running around in my skivvies. I didn't feel lucky. When I got back to the home, one of the older girls laughed and said I could sew the front and back together and make a nice skirt. I didn't laugh. What *was* funny was that while the officer was talking to the staff members, I ran out the back door. It was over an hour before I got caught again. A state patrolman found me by the Massachusetts turnpike. He took me to the station and eventually back to the group home after they figured out where I was supposed to be.

Not long after this, my Grandpa Caravelli passed away. I loved him so much and they would not let me go to the funeral. I thought my heart was breaking into a million pieces. The only man I ever trusted was gone and I was not there to say goodbye. I was out of control so they restrained me all day long. While I was restrained, a male staff member kept grabbing my vagina. I was screaming that he was touching me, but no one came. There was another male staff member in there, and although he didn't do anything to me, he didn't try to stop the other guy either. Finally, after I screamed for what seemed like an eternity, they sent two women into my room to take over. That staff member was later fired after three other girls came forward with molestation complaints.

Later that week my mom was supposed to come for me to have a home visit, but she didn't show up. That same day the director refused to let me talk to my boyfriend. On top of the other events of the week, that was the culminating factor and I started throwing rocks at the director. They tried to restrain me but not before one of the rocks hit her in the head. An officer took me to the police station and charged me with assault and battery with a deadly weapon. Some time later, when I went to court, the charges were dropped. I now think they were trying to make a case to move me to a different, more-restricted section of the home. I remember the new section had a glass window and I kept seeing all of these bugs outside of the window. I started thinking that they were going to attack and kill me.

Back to the psychiatric ward I went.

Deaconess, Thirteen to Sixteen Years

I first met Mr. Gordon in the psychiatric ward. He was the man in charge at the Deaconess home. He came to the hospital and I was unmerciful with my jabs about his tall frame and flaming red hair. I seem to remember "Jack O' Lantern Freak" as one name. I looked right at him and said, "There is no fucking way I am going with you. Over your dead body." He allowed me to ramble on for a while and then he looked right at me and said, "I like you. You are a good candidate for my facility. I'll see you soon."

When the social worker showed up a few weeks later to take me to Deaconess, he didn't restrain me. He must have been new. I was free as a bird and I ran like the Roadrunner. I ran until my knees were physically buckling, but unfortunately I ran right into a duck pond. They had to fish me out, clean me up, and off to the home I went.

Mr. Gordon and the program director Joyce met me at the door. I was brought into the home in an ambulance on a stretcher. Mr. Gordon simply said, "Fancy entrance," and then reiterated, "I told you I would see you in a couple of weeks." Turns out Mr. Gordon was a man of his word. I was intrigued by him and our relationship was to bloom into the perfect example of love/hate.

Deaconess housed women from ages 11-22 and focused on rehabilitation.[4] I was to remain at Deaconess off and on for the next three years. My first week there was rough. Someone set me up with a fork. I was in bed around 8:30 p.m. and a staff member came into my room to look in my cubby, a skinny locker where we could put our things. I had only been there a week so I think I had Fun Dip and an outfit or two. She sent me to timeout but I had no idea why. I was there for half an hour before she came back and said, "Tell me about the fork, Ava."

---

[4]
 The goal at the Fall River Deaconess Home "is to develop in each young woman the social and academic skills necessary to engage fully and freely in the traditional life systems of family, community, school, and work."
http://deaconesshome.org/about-us/

Apparently, they count the silverware after every meal and a fork was missing that night after dinner. I had no idea what she was talking about. She left and came back in another half-hour and asked the same thing. This went on all night. At 7:30 a.m. she gathered all of the residents together and asked us about the fork. After a while she told everyone that I had stolen it. Everyone was mad at me because they had to stand there for so long. My caseworker told me to admit stealing the fork so everyone could move past the situation. I lied and said I did it, and when they asked why, I lied again and said I wanted to hurt myself. I didn't steal that fork but I did not want to go back to timeout all night long again.

I did settle in to the routines but I remained my own worst enemy. Our group meetings were on

Wednesdays and they were very organized. Everyone attended. Picture 40 staff members with Mr. Gordon sitting in a circle of chairs and all the residents in the middle on the floor. We were each permitted to have one discrepancy and one request a week.

I was a big gay-basher at these meetings from the very start. Phrases like "don't touch me I don't want to catch that" were common comments from me. I did it just to be mean. Toward the end of my stay, I remember passing a note to a friend. In the note, I shared that I thought the reason why I cut gay people down so much was because I thought I might be gay. Miss Anatoli, one of the teachers, caught the note and read it. It got brought up in the meeting and everyone in the group who was gay was allowed to say something to me. I found out how wrong I was and how much hurt I had caused over the years. I just cried and said I was sorry. I deserved hearing what they had to say and it changed me somehow. This wasn't the only lesson I learned at Deaconess.

I learned mostly because of the firm, yet fair treatment of one man, Mr. Gordon, and the influence he had over this group home. From the very beginning of my stay, Mr. Gordon always seemed to have my back, whether I deserved it or not.

Still, I was angry all the time and caused a great deal of trouble. If a resident stirred up trouble at the house, they were required to carry around a spark plug (sparking trouble). I had the spark plug for a year and a half. I always requested giving it to someone else but Mr. Gordon always refused. He somehow knew I could do better.

Bloom Where Planted

I remember on occasion we had to have a moment of silence when we were done eating. You had to look down, not talk, just stay still. That was not an easy thing for me to do and when I looked up at the clock to see how much longer, a staff member sitting across from me told me to put my eyes down. At first, I did, but this time I couldn't help but look at the clock. After some verbal back and forth, the staff member told me to go to timeout. I told the her, "Fuck you, I'm not going to timeout." Of course they came to take me there, but I ran under the tables and crawled on all fours trying to get away. When they caught me, they restrained me for six hours. Every time I told them to "fuck off" they pulled my arms up higher behind my back and tightened the restraints. When they finally let me go, my shoulder cracked and hurt unmercifully for days.

During our group meeting the following Wednesday, I spoke up when Mr. Gordon asked me what I thought was wrong. I shared that after six hours in restraints, pulling my arms up my back caused me to have pain in my arm still. Mr. Gordon stopped the meeting and asked who the staff members were. In front of all the group, he said if he ever heard of that happening again to any one of the residents, those staff members would be fired. Up until that very minute, I had never had a man stick up for me when someone did something wrong. This would not be the last time Mr. Gordon stuck up for me.

I remember one time my weekly request was to find my half-brothers. I was crying while I was asking, and I remember my leg wouldn't stop shaking. I had found a company that would try to locate missing people for $150. Of course, I didn't have that money but Mr. Gordon requested it from the office and paid for them to be found. The company never was successful; my half-brothers were lost in the system, but Mr. Gordon tried just the same.

Another time I was on Run Away Policy (RAP) and my weekly request was to go for a walk. Mr. Gordon said, "So you are on RAP and you are requesting a walk?" He okayed it and I was given my regular clothes and my sneakers. He gave me his watch and said, "You have half an hour." I came back in 29 minutes.

He trusted me but I don't know why because I was a runner.

One time I ran away and stayed at two lesbians' home. I was walking down the street and I asked them if

I could stay with them. They said, "Yes," and I stayed at their place for two weeks. They were nice to me. I must have mentioned where I was to a friend or something because after a few weeks, the staff from Deaconess came for me.

Another time I ran on a Wednesday. This turned out to be stupid because the place was fully staffed in the middle of the week. I hid under someone's porch and it took three staff members to pull me out. They dragged me back, kicking and screaming. I knew better than to run on a Wednesday again.

The older I got, the more privileges I was given. After three years at Deaconess, I got summer employment. I had two jobs that summer. One of them was at a Jewish nursing home and the other was in a doctor's office. I remember making beds in the Jewish home where this one lady just hated me. She would call me names and refuse to let me in the room to clean. One time we had put on a production of *Alice in Wonderland* at the home and I was a frog footman, Tweedledum, and a mouse. When I went to work I showed the woman a picture of me as a mouse, and she said, "I always knew you were a rat, Ava." After that, for some reason that I still don't know, we started to get along. I ended up getting fired because some other girl locked people in the closet; they let us both go and I never saw the woman again.

After that, I filed papers at a doctor's office. I was required to make phone calls and set up appointments. One random call was to a boy who sounded around my age. His name was Stephen. I ended up making the appointment and calling him back.

It wasn't long before he became important to me and I decided to run away and see him.

I now lived in Prospect House at Deaconess, which housed older residents who had served some time and were not getting into as much trouble. Therefore, the staff-to-resident ratio was much smaller at this campus. I decided to go see Stephen. My first opportunity to run was when my mom and my sister came to visit. It was never hard to talk my mom into something that I wanted to do. At this point, manipulating my mom had become an art form. She carried around so much guilt that she would do just about anything I asked. I told her that I wanted to run away and use her car, to which she answered a quick, "No." After I repeatedly informed her that I would go anyway, and I wouldn't be safe, she finally agreed. My sister had fallen asleep on the couch and my mom asked a staff member to get a bottle of nail polish from the desk. As soon as the staff member left, my mom opened the window and the screen and gave me the keys so I could take the car. The plan was that I would park the car down the road and go on foot. This was a great plan except for one small detail; I was 16 years old and had been in lockdown for many years. I had no idea how to drive.

I got in the car, but I didn't know where to put the key, so I sat there for some time trying to make the car move. I finally figured out that you had to put the key in the ignition and turn it. I had the accelerator to the floor but wasn't moving. When I pulled the drive shaft into reverse, the car flew into the car behind me. I pulled the shaft to drive, still with the accelerator to the floor, and the car lurched forward and smashed into the car in front of me. I slammed the drive shaft into reverse and again smashed into the car behind me.

After the second try in drive, I was successful in getting out of the parallel parking space and thought I was home-free. However, I didn't know how to steer and with the accelerator floored, I went straight and crashed into the front porch of the house across the street from the group home.

Needless to say, the porch was shattered and I moved the slab of cement that had been in front of the house about 100 feet. Even though my ribs were killing me and I had some trouble breathing without hurting, I dug my way out of the debris and ran. The only thing I heard was someone yelling, "Come back here you little bitch," but I never turned around to see who it was. I think it is important to note that I was later told there was a man getting out of a nearby car with his newborn baby. Had I been just a few yards over, I might have killed them.

I stayed with some lady for three weeks. I have no memory of who she was or how I met her. I watched "Dumb and Dumber" and "Teenage Mutant Ninja Turtles" over and over because that was all she had at her place. The very first chance I had, I met up with Stephen. We met at his apartment but the apartment above his was not rented so we went up there together. I told him I wanted to have sex and that it was not my first time. I don't know why I lied.

The only thing I remember about my first experience with sex was that was on the cement floor of an apartment and I kept moving backward across the floor. It hurt so bad and I wanted to get away. I backed up all the way into the wall, hit my head, and just waited until it ended. I lay there until I fell asleep. When I woke up, some guy was standing over me and there was blood everywhere. Apparently he was the landlord and he was not happy. I just ran. That was the only time we had sex.

I got my first tattoo shortly after that experience. Stephen's friend Junebug knew how to give homemade tattoos. We were at Junebug's place; he lit a Rice-A-Roni box on fire and scraped the ashes from the box into a little bottle cap. Then he took a needle and thread, put the needle in the ashes, and began poking small holes, over and over. I got a hollow cross on my upper right shoulder.

Bloom Where Planted

After three weeks, I left the lady's house and stayed with one of Stephen's friends. I needed money so I called my mom for help. She gave me clothes and money but she also set me up; she called Deaconess and they came to the house. When Stephen answered the door, the police said they were looking for Ava so I hid in the back room. I tried to get out through the fire escape, but I couldn't get the window open. When the police came after me I threw a lamp and hit one of the police officers in the head.

I was charged with six different counts: driving without a license, driving to endanger, two accounts of assault with a deadly weapon, damage, and hit and run (the house). They put me in handcuffs and took me to the station. There they handcuffed me to a bench until the paperwork was filled out. Then my Department of

Children and Family Services (DCF) worker came and got me and took me to the Brockton YMCA.

I spoke to Mr. Gordon while writing this chapter. I gave my name to his administrative assistant, and after hearing my name for the first time in about 16 years, he took the call. The first thing he said was, "I'm sitting in the room where you drove that car into the porch. Ironically, we ended up buying that house. Maybe we should name it after you, Ava!" He divulged some of his philosophy about working with children, "that things have a tendency to work out. It may look awful in the beginning, but somehow it gets better." He shared that he always had faith in me and I shared that I felt like he always had my back. I told him of my appreciation for all that he had done for me and he said, "When you work with kids, you have to remember there is always another side to the story. You were able to take information and make the right decisions and after all, that's what it's about: learning from your mistakes."

Now, yes, but not then.

Brockton YMCA, Sixteen Years

Many people don't know that there is a lock-up facility at the YMCA in Brockton, Massachusetts. It was so crowded but I was only there for three or four weeks. Almost immediately, I was introduced to the director and I spit in her face. That added an additional charge, assault and battery, to my already lengthy list.

The system was strict and unbending. I was to take three-minute showers. Shaving was always supervised, no exception. I remember one girl who insisted upon defecating in her socks and putting them in the dryer with all of our clothes. We were required to wear uniforms, but it got to the point where we would have to borrow clothes from the boys' unit because we would run out of clean clothes in our unit. That girl was not right.

I did have some good memories from the Y. For some reason we were permitted to crochet in the common area. We were given hooks and yarn. For the first time in my life, I learned a positive skill. Not long after, I figured out that I could earn extra snacks for braiding hair. In my unit, I was the only white girl who knew how to braid hair so I had a lot of "customers." The food was great too and I finally began to gain weight. We had a pet mouse in the kitchen named Mr. Jangles. He made me happy.

Bloom Where Planted

I think I loved a girl named Kendall while I was there. This was the first girlfriend I ever had. We started out in the same room but that didn't last long; they soon separated us, but not far enough. We ended up in rooms next to each other and we would communicate through the heater vent. I would fall asleep with my head on that vent many nights.

There were bad times there, as well. I recall several incidents during my short stay when I was charged with starting riots. They had a timeout room with mats on the floor. I was in there many times. We had a school, but it didn't take me long to figure out that if someone called the teacher a "bitch," they were sent upstairs. After the first day, I never spent another day in school.

This was only a temporary holding facility for me until my trial. When the time came, they transported me to the courthouse. There were several people in attendance on my behalf: Joyce from Deaconess, a probation officer, a Department of Youth Services (DYS) worker, and a Department of Social Services (DSS) worker. During the court hearing, Deaconess made it very clear that they wanted me to go back. I told the judge, "No way in hell" was I going back to that place.

Maybe I didn't want people to care about me, especially Mr. Gordon. Maybe I just wanted to be a number, not a person with a name. Either way, I asked to be committed to the DYS, which meant back to the YMCA as a temporary holding facility. Based on the seven charges that had been filed against me, they committed me until I was 18. I was not allowed to get a driver's permit until I was 18 and I had to be 21 for the license. I was also given a sentence of 1,000 hours of community service and fined $1,000 in restitution.

They put me in a belly chain[5] and transported me back to Brockton. On the way there, I somehow managed to get out of the handcuffs and when they stopped at the boys' unit to let a prisoner out, they discovered that I was out of my hand shackles so they charged me with being AWOL. I didn't care. I only wanted to see Kendall again, so I was glad to go back. What I hadn't foreseen was that I was only there for a few months before they transferred me to a lock-up

---

[5]
Many times used when transporting prisoners, "consisting of a chain around the waist, to which the prisoner's hands may be chained or cuffed. Sometimes the ankles are also connected by means of longer chains."
https://en.wikipedia.org/wiki/Belly_chain_(restraint)

facility in Dorchester, MA. It was a maximum-security lock-up for minors.

Dorchester, Sixteen to Seventeen Years

There were so many people at Dorchester. My unit had four girls to a room and was tiny. There were two-minute showers except when there was no hot water. When the water ran cold, which was often, I stood in a bucket; the other girls would heat up water in the microwave and pour the hot water over me as I washed.

There were some good things at Dorchester. There was a pool and I could go swimming if I stayed out of trouble. Although I was in trouble a great deal of the time, I really liked it when I was permitted to swim, mostly because of a girl named Andrea. She was the first girl I was intimate with and it usually happened in the pool. She loved me so much.

My mom came to see me a few times while I was in this facility. One time she brought me a pair of Jordans but someone stole them shortly after.

I didn't mind staying there, but that didn't stop me from escaping. I honestly don't remember how I got out of that place, but when I got out, I called my cousin Toni. We knew each other from the YMCA lock-up facility and she took me in for a while. I don't know how long I was out, but there are distinct memories of aimlessly walking around the streets of Boston.

I did find Kendall while I was out. She lived in a town close to the city and I stayed with her for a while, but something had changed. For some reason, we just couldn't find on the outside what we had on the inside.

Maybe it was a sense of doing something wrong, or fighting back against the system, but whatever it was, it was gone.

Rotenberg Educational Center, Seventeen to Just Shy of Eighteen Years

It was the summer before 9-11 when they caught me and sent me to Rotenberg.[6] This lock-up for juveniles was a high maximum-security facility. From the outside, it looked like a castle. I remember walking in and thinking it was so beautiful outside, but I was entering the dungeon of this castle and it was not a fairy tale. Clad in chains, I walked through the doors, and

---

[6] When I googled this facility, this is the article that came up "This controversial Massachusetts facility is the last in the country to use electric shock on students."
http://www.masslive.com/news/index.ssf/2016/07/inside_judge_rotenberg_center.html

they closed for the next year of my life. The yard was double-fenced with barbed wire coiled around the top. All of the windows were barred. Girls at this facility ranged in age from 15 to 21 years and many were on their way to jail.

There were four girls to a room and I knew no one. The staff was more transient than in any other facility I had been in prior. The residents didn't leave though, we stayed; and the longer I stayed, the worse my behavior got. I didn't know anyone and I was so angry. I was in timeout most of the time. The timeout room had scratchy, wooden walls. I was in there what seemed like constantly, walking in circles, hitting my head against the walls until I bled. I have scars on my forehead from beating my head so many times on the walls in this facility. I would scream and scream and try to get everyone to act the same. Causing riots was a goal. Anything to get out.

I kept hitting on every girl in that place. It didn't matter who it was or what they tried to do to stop me, I just kept at it. And stop me they tried. I had an incessant need to try and have sexual relations with anyone, everyone I came in contact with. I was put on a "talking ban," forbidden to talk to anyone. If I talked, they immediately threw me in timeout. I was the only one who showered alone. I was confined to my own room because my roommates could not deal with me.

Maybe because I didn't want to be alone or maybe because I wanted the attention, I was constantly causing a scene in my room. I remember one kind woman on the staff brought in a 10-inch, black-and-white television and let me watch it until I fell asleep.

That seemed to help in my bedroom. In the timeout room, she would set a sound machine outside of the door. It had various settings for rain or waves and calmed me down so I could eventually fall asleep. She was nice to me but so many of the staff members were not. Many of the staff members were performing sex acts with the inmates. I took advantage of this "perk" a time or two in order to get out of timeout or get extra snacks. It was common practice on the inside.

I never ran away from Rotenberg. It was not possible. I devised a plan to escape another way. I made up a story about a guy named Tony who lived inside my belly. I told anyone who would listen about Tony. Finally, they put me in an ambulance and took me to the hospital in Springfield. I told them in the hospital that it would be a waste to X-ray me because he would hide in my anal cavity and they wouldn't be able to see him. They admitted me to the psych ward. I was restrained the entire time. They used a Papoose Board[7] to completely immobilize me.

I felt confined against my will and scared, the same feelings I had when Charlie, my mom's boyfriend, used to hold me down when I was little. It was horrible and I was out of my mind. When I called the nurse a "bitch," she slapped me across the face while I was in restraints. There, no one listened to anything I said. It didn't take me long to figure out it was worse in the ward than it was at Rotenberg, so I got my act together and was sent back.

---

[7] https://www.universalmedicalinc.com/all-products/patient-positioning/pediatric-immobilizers/papoose-boards.html?gclid=EAIaIQobChMIsPf_hKjk1wIVkIizCh0QCASGEAAYASAAEgKXQ_D_BwE

Bloom Where Planted

The required weekly group work was a joke to me. We received a weekly allowance for doing chores and from that, we were required to pay $1.00 and "send" it to our victims. Our victims were the people whom we had wronged in our past and I had plenty. So we sat in a circle every week, said what we were sorry for, and made monetary atonement for our wrongdoings. We also had regular AA meetings. I thought it was funny to listen to the same people tell the same stories, every week. It just never changed. It got to the point where people were glorifying their behavior when they were drunk or high. In my mind, an addict has to want to be clean in order to achieve sobriety, not recognized for exaggerated, half-truth adventures. And they have to hit rock bottom.

During the week we got to choose between Bible study or physical activity. I chose Bible study every time. I made that choice because I hated physical activity. It was during one of these Bible studies that I accepted God into my heart, although at the time, I'm not sure I believed He would hear me or want me.

My mom lived three hours away, so she could only come every few months. Three months before I turned 18, I was eligible for release. There was a big meeting with my therapist, caseworker, probation officer, psychologist, DSS representative, DYS representative, the program director, and my mom. The group consensus was that I could go home on house arrest for three months until I turned 18, or be recommitted to the DYS until I was 21. My mom agreed to take me for three months into her custody. She did not wait after the meeting for me, so the caseworker drove me home.

Equipped with an electronic ankle bracelet and the clothes on my back, I headed toward uncertainty in a home that had no meaning.

Chapter 3 – Almost Eighteen

At home, my mom and Dan had separated and it didn't take long for my mom's new boyfriend, Andy, and I to butt heads. I just didn't know what my mom saw in him. To me, he looked like a troll. Not only was his body like a troll's, short and squatty, but he also had long hair and old plastic glasses. I don't think he worked or if he did, I didn't know about it. He was always there, watching and lurking. He hated my friends and made it very clear that we were bad news and headed nowhere. My mom acted so differently when he was around. She was noticeably paranoid that he would take an interest in me and was extremely verbal about warning me to cover up.

My sister didn't get along with Andy either, but he treated her differently. At one point she was getting bullied in the neighborhood. She stole Andy's knife and threatened the girls who were picking on her. The police were called. While Andy was talking to the police up front, Trisha threw the knife out the back window. She told those girls she would kill them if they messed with her anymore. When the police left, Andy yelled at Trisha but blamed me. He always blamed me for her actions. She didn't care at all. The bullying stopped after her threats so to her, it was worth it. As for me, I knew I needed to get out of there before Andy's quiet, under-his-breath threats turned into actions.

After about two weeks of living at home, I decided that I'd had enough. I knew I had to get the fuck out of there. I called JoJo, a girl whom I had met while in lock-up, and told her I needed a place to stay. I cut off the ankle bracelet and as we passed over the bridge into Boston, I threw it into the water. I later had to tell my parole officer but I didn't care at the time.

I would find out that to "stay" with JoJo meant constantly moving to different hotels and different houses of people who I did not know. At first, I liked moving around. JoJo was dating a guy named "Big T." He was the biggest, darkest man I had ever seen. For a while, I really connected with them. We would go shopping and hang out together all the time.

It took me awhile to realize that JoJo was a prostitute. It may be hard to believe, but I was relatively naive about the act of sex even at almost eighteen years old. Up until this point in my life, I had little experience with actually having sex. I didn't lose my virginity until I was sixteen and I was locked up immediately after that for another year and a half.

Bloom Where Planted

Wherever we would go, Big T was always yelling at JoJo not to look other guys in the eyes or she would be "out of pocket."[8] Although it seems so dysfunctional now, then it felt like security from an unknown evil. In some twisted way, it seemed to me like he wanted to keep us "safe."

Big T would drop JoJo off downtown Boston every night. One night she dressed me up as a mirror image of herself, really trashy-looking, and Big T dropped both of us off. I didn't know what was happening. Out of nowhere, JoJo told me that I had to have sex with strangers and give them blow jobs. It wasn't long before some guy pulled up and wanted me to get into his car. I said, "Fuck no." That was not what I was prepared for and I didn't know what to do. My

---

[8] Another pimp could take the money from the score and the prostitute would have to work harder to pay back the money their pimp lost. Time is money.

reaction prompted a big argument between me and JoJo because she didn't want to get into trouble with Big T. She was afraid of him. We argued but somehow I avoided getting into any cars that night or any other.

    The next night we all went to a party. It wasn't long before the argument from the night before followed us there. We fought verbally until it escalated into a physical fight and JoJo ended up punching me in the face. Simultaneously, Big T started in verbally. He wanted me to join JoJo on the streets. He kept saying over and over how nobody loved me or cared about me back home and that he was the only one who could take care of me. I felt so isolated. Somehow I ended up in a back room alone with Big T, a lesbian, and a mentally challenged young boy. Big T told me, "You need to have sex with that girl." I had been with girls before but

I could not comprehend what was happening. To be forced to have sex on demand with a random female felt like a nightmare. Suddenly I had the courage to yell, "I'm not doing that." He got louder and louder, screaming in my face. I cried and kept saying, "No. No. No."

I just wanted to go home.

It wasn't long before he said, "Fuck you," one last time, then raped me in front of those people. He forced me down onto my knees and began to push my head and mouth onto his penis. My mouth is small and it couldn't accommodate the size of his male parts. I screamed and cried and kept yelling, "No!" He threw me on the bed face-down and I felt his massive penis inside of me. It felt like I was being ripped in half. He held my mouth closed while he raped me from behind.

I went numb. I shut down mentally and imagined myself anywhere but where I was. When he finished he said to clean up. I could barely close my legs from the pain.

Chapter 4 – The Dance

Some people shut down completely when they are raped. Not me. I moved back in with my mom for a few weeks and I tried to have sex with as many people as would pay attention to me. I met people off phone chat lines or people who lived in the projects near my mom's house. It didn't matter if they were male or female. There were times when one person would be going out the back and another person would be coming in the front. I loved the attention and I felt loved in a sick way. It was almost like an addiction. I got "high" off controlling people with my body. It felt like I was in control of myself and others. I never prostituted myself for sex but I sorely mistreated myself. When I think back, I can only say that at the time, I didn't think I deserved any better.

I remember one guy I met off a chat line, named Andy. I agreed to go "out" with him. When he showed up at my mom's house, I was packed and ready to go to his place and hang out with him for the weekend. My mom opened the door to see a heavyset, 40-something-year-old woman. She had a dozen roses in her hand and said, "I am here to pick up Ava." My mom and I just looked at each other, confused, and I said, "Oh well," and went anyway. I stayed with Andy for a few weeks and I really had fun. She taught me how to drive and showed me how to cook. Unfortunately, I ended up getting a very bad kidney infection and went back to my mom's house.

Dancing

Bloom Where Planted

As soon as I could get out of Tonya's house I did. I moved in with a girl named Ginny. She was a dancer and lived with a guy who looked exactly like Snoop Dogg. Ginny taught me to dance. I made a lot of money. It changed my life.

Dancing seemed glamorous. I did not realize that dancing is very competitive. At the time, it never crossed my mind that it was dangerous. I know differently now.

It's not like Demi Moore in "Striptease" where they are all friends. I think in that movie they even babysat Demi's daughter a few times when she had to work. That was not my experience. In my experience, few dancers made friends and if they did, they were often friends because rent is cheaper when split or they had drug dependencies and needed the friend for a fix.

For the most part, dancers stayed to themselves. Why would you want to be friends with other girls in a strip club? Many are drug addicts or like to fight and get in trouble. Most of the time, strippers work against each other. Every guy in the dance club is looked at as a money sign. It is not a good idea to become friends with people who are taking your potential income.

I had a fascination with dancing. As it turned out, it is not easy.

First Dance

When I walked into the Satin Doll for the first time, it was overwhelming. The room was dim and my eyes took a minute to adjust to the low lighting. The stage was front and center and I thought to myself, "What the fuck am I doing here?" All of the girls were staring like I was about to steal their meal ticket. All of the men were looking at me like lions, ready to pounce on unsuspecting prey. The manager took me into his office to fill out paperwork. I gave him my identification. I was 18 years and three days old.

I walked into the dressing room and looked around awkwardly at all of the girls, veterans, and I thought again, "What the fuck am I doing here?" They all knew what they were doing. They were already established. Who was I to think I could, or should, be a part of what they already knew?

I remember being so excited about the outfit that I had picked out for my audition. It was from Frederick's of Hollywood. A white bra, white thong, and a sheer white flowing jacket. The excitement and security I had felt earlier that day when I showed the outfit to my mom was crushed as I looked around at the other girls. They were all dressed in provocative outfits that called out to men. All of a sudden, I realized that I looked out of place. As soon as silent doubt crept into my mind, I heard my name being called from the stage.

I had two songs to prove I was good enough to be there: to dance in their club. When I stepped onto the stage, my heart was pounding so hard I felt it in my chest. The music was so loud my ears were ringing. The lights that earlier were so dim were now in my eyes, bright and blinding. My legs shook as I walked to the pole and clung to it. The pole was a needed crutch providing support for my legs and comfort for my hands. I did my best to dance and make eye contact with the men who sat longingly around the stage. I was afraid of not being good enough and not getting hired. That they would reject me. Send me away.

The second song ended. I left the stage I heard the manager say, "Congratulations," and once again I said to myself, "What the fuck am I doing here?"

An older, well-dressed man caught my attention while I was on stage. He repeatedly handed me $5 bills as I danced. In my new white work clothes, I went over to him and sat down. He was kind. He told me I was beautiful. He told me I was angelic. Never before had anyone told me such things about myself. My frail 90-pound frame danced in front of him and I did a few lap dances for him during the rest of the night. By the time I left, he had given me $900 and it was then that I realized I could get men to pay me to feed my emotional needs: to be loved, to be needed, to be wanted. I was hooked.

<u>Clubs</u>

Different clubs charge different fees. Generally, you pay a cut to the manager, the DJ, the bar backs, the bartender, and the servers. Some bars require that you pay all of the people and some require paying just some of them. Either way, you have to work twice as hard to walk out with money. Sometimes I would tip the bouncer or the VIP guy (a man who sits in the VIP area and watches the camera to make sure no one is doing anything they shouldn't be doing) an extra fifty bucks to tell me which guys to go sit with. The VIP guys usually pay attention to who is spending money and can give you a heads-up to who to sit next to at the bar. I guess in a way they were my "friends" at work.

I will admit that I was the "look-out" for another girl. If a girl decided to perform illegal sexual activities, I would keep watch to make sure no one would see. For example, if someone wanted to give a blow job for $400, I would watch for the VIP guy and she would give me half of what she made. I would make a quick $200 and I didn't have to do anything sexual myself.

There are different types of strip clubs. Most common is topless or nude but there are bikini bars as well. The physical layout of the room depends on the bar. The stage is almost always located in the middle of the bar. There are chairs lined along the stage. In my experience, the men in these clubs like to get as close as possible to see all of the dancer's body parts close up. Looking back at this now, it was so degrading. Nasty men inches from my vagina. I can still feel their breath.

The dressing rooms are located in the back. In some clubs, girls are able to do "table dances" where the girl dances for the guy out in the main area and gets tips in her G-string. "Private" dances happen in the VIP area, which is normally secluded away from the front. In some clubs, private dances occur on couches while in others there are chairs separated with dividers. Some clubs have a champagne room and you pay by the hour. You can get drinks and a girl (or girls) for the hour or longer, depending on your wallet. The price for a girl can be $300 to $500 depending on the club. The bottom line is, no matter what you're looking for, if you have the money to pay for it, you can usually find a club that will make it happen.

I remember one club had a dungeon in it. I asked the owner if I could see what was in the dungeon. He took me in there with another girl. There were all kinds of apparatus or "toys" if you will, although I would hesitate to think that any of them were fun. In the middle of this dark room, a table hung from the ceiling. It was a thick board suspended by some kind of heavy chains with a sheet of glass that hung a few feet above it. I asked the manager what the fuck that thing was used for and he informed me that the table was for men to lie on. I was confused so I asked more questions. A man would lie on this slab of wood with just enough space for himself between the wood and glass. Then a woman would come in and get on top of that glass and piss or shit. I was so disgusted and intrigued all at the same time.

Clientele

You can tell when a guy walks in if he is going to spend money or not. I like to put the men in these clubs into several different categories.

- The drinking guy will sit at a table or at the bar and will have a few one-dollar bills on the table. Sometimes, but not always, he will tip the girl who is dancing but will rarely ask for any private dancers for himself.
- Some guys are full of themselves. The ego guy is well-dressed and will have a pile of ones. Usually ego guy just wants to talk and have someone pay attention to him.
- Guys who come in wearing sweat pants; now this guy is coming in ready for business. He is a veteran. He comes in for a lap dance. He is usually a pig. Sweat-pants guy comes in and

goes right to the back for private dances. He knows what he wants and doesn't waste time getting it.

The managers can be just as piggish as the customers. They feel as though you owe them something. It is not uncommon for girls to give an occasional blow job to the manager to get out of paying fees. Fortunately for me, paying the fees was not a problem. You have to pay to work; the more you make, the more you "tip out."

This was the first time I had my own money and I thought I was happy. I felt like I had freedom for the first time in my life. This was a façade because at the same time, I was feeling the effect of the rape. I was having sex with anyone who was even remotely kind to me. If anyone showed me even the least bit of interest, I mistook the shallow attention as love and acceptance. Although I thought I was in control, I was so wrong.

The Downward Spiral

Ginny and I smoked a lot of pot and I knew she did ecstasy but I didn't want to do any hard drugs. When I turned 18, I had taken myself off of all prescription drugs and I didn't want to get caught up in them again. I didn't want to feel out of control. When she asked me to try ecstasy I lied and told her I had a heart murmur.

We got into a nice routine of dancing at the club and then going out to our favorite clubs after the Satin Doll closed. We would get to the clubs around 3 a.m. and just dance and dance and dance. I remember sitting on a smelly old couch in a club called Therapy after hours with some guy. He asked me if I wanted free X. Ginny overheard and she came over and told him I couldn't because of my heart. I assured her I would only do half a pill and that I would be fine. By the end of the night I had taken four. I went back to Ginny's house with her and her boyfriend. I had no cares at all. We were all watching Sponge Bob together and I was jumping and twirling around. I was just so happy to be there.

The false happiness was short-lived and things got progressively worse. I was dancing and smoking pot and taking X every night. It wasn't long before Ginny's boyfriend started saying I had to give him half of what I made. One night he put a gun to my face and demanded that I give him half of my money. I simply said, "Pull the trigger. I don't have anything to live for anyway."

He smashed the gun into my cheek and said to get out. So I did.

I went to stay with my stepdad Dan. He had a girlfriend at the time and they fought constantly. She always had bruises on her face. He never touched me for the two weeks I was there. I don't know why but for that I am thankful.

I met up with my second cousin Ben. When my sister Trisha and I were younger, Ben's mom owned a laundromat. She always had Lemonheads in a jar by the door and we would stop in and grab a handful. Even then, we knew that Ben was "off." When my aunt couldn't run the business anymore, she gave the business to her son. He opened a pet shop in the back of the store. The laundromat was eventually shut down because the police found out that Ben had started torturing animals in the back room.

Ben owned a rooming house and I moved in. The proverbial "fire into the flame." The house smelled like urine all the time because people would get drunk and urinate anywhere. But the rent was $150 a week and I was pulling in $3,000 to $4,000 a night at the Satin Doll so the rent was nothing.

As I think about this now, I could have lived in a nice place with the money I was making. But because I timed out of the system, I was immediately turned out on my own. There was no transition into the world and I had no idea how to react. I had no experience with working in the "real" world so I did not know how to budget, save, or spend in a "normal" manner. I ate every meal out or ordered delivery. I made a great deal of money and I spent a great deal of money.

In Ben's rooming house, each floor was its own apartment. There was a kitchen on my floor but that didn't matter because the only thing I ate was pizza or McDonald's. Everyone had to share a bathroom. There was no door on the bathroom and we put garbage bags inside and around the tub because of the black mold and so you didn't get fungus on your feet. It was a crack house with beds everywhere and most tenants were also heroin addicts. I had two beds in my room and a dresser. I loved writing graffiti on my walls and whenever I had someone over, they wrote messages on my walls as well. Ecstasy and pot were on my daily list of things to do. I was constantly high. Ben warned me not to open the door and share anything with people but when someone knocked at the door and wanted a roach I gave it to them. It wasn't long until there were constant knocks at my door.

During this haze I met up with a girl named Anna. She had run away from lock-up,[9] and at that time in my life, I thought my place was better than being on the streets. I invited her to stay with me and it wasn't long before I had her doing drugs. I didn't force her but I didn't stop her either. She told me she was eighteen but she lied.

My cousin Ben soon found out that Anna was living in the room with me and he kept picking at her for rent. I told him many times I would pay her rent but he just wore her down and she began to sleep with him to

---

9
    Lock-up was referred to as "The Training School" in Rhode Island. It is a juvenile detention facility. Children under eighteen go to this facility waiting trial and until they decide if they will try you as a juvenile or an adult.

pay for the room. She complained of sodomy to me more than once.

One night I was woken from a dead sleep by a punch in the face. Anna had white powder all over her face. She had watched a Keebler Elf on TV and was sure that I was an elf. Her hallucinations were out of control and she took out knives to throw them. It took a long time to bring her down.

I had been rolling[10] for ten days straight. Much of the time spent in that room was a blur. I was bringing home random people, doing Special K[11] and GSB[12] on a regular basis. I knew it had to stop.

10

Ecstacy (methylenedioxymethylamphetamine) MDMA is a 'psychedelic amphetamine' that has gained popularity over the past 20 years because of its ability to produce strong feelings of comfort, empathy, and connection to others. It most frequently comes in tablet form, although it is occasionally sold in capsules or as powder. It is most frequently used orally and rarely snorted

https://www.urbandictionary.com/define.php?term=Ecstasy

11

Bloom Where Planted

I had to quit or die and so I stopped everything. I had been taking drugs of one type or another every day for two years. When I quit, I stayed in my room alone for three days, feeling like I was being jabbed with pins and needles. It was three months before I felt "normal" again.

By divine intervention I knew it was time to go. I just knew it was not safe to stay in the rooming house anymore. My cousin found out that Anna and I were talking about leaving. Obviously, he was not going to let his "toy" Anna go without a fight. For some reason, I

Special K (<u>Ketamine</u>) is often obtained by breaking into animal hospitals, this liquid-state tranquilizer can be poured over a <u>mirror</u>, dried, and diced into a <u>powder</u> and snorted.
https://www.urbandictionary.com/define.php?term=special%20k

12
GHB (gamma hydroxybutyrate) is illegally produced in home basement labs, usually in the form of a **liquid** that has no odor or color. It is known as a designer drug because it is specifically made for the purpose of getting people high
https://www.urbandictionary.com/define.php?term=ghb

tried to call my best friend, Carina, but Dan ripped the phone from my hand and out of the wall and smashed it. Anna left in a hurry and was in such a panic she got in a car accident, and was sent back to lock-up. I was happy she had lived.

Chapter 5 - Tommy

When people hear mention of the Kings Inn, they might assume it is a venue fit for a king. However, this establishment is a run-down building filled with middle-aged strippers and the occasional hot one (like myself of course). It was at this club located in Dartmouth, Massachusetts that my life changed drastically when I met the father of my beautiful daughter.

When I first saw Tommy he was sitting at the bar in the Kings Inn. I went over to talk to him and he immediately said, "I'm not going into the back and I'm not doing any dances with you." When he wasn't interested in me, I was even more intrigued. After all, I was in a bar designed to make me more appealing to the clientele. I don't know if it was because he was cute or because he turned me down, but I liked him right away.

I met his rude remark with, "Who the hell said I want to dance with you," to which he responded, "You are too young for me. Get out of here!" I grabbed his phone and added my phone number in his address book. He called me a few days later and I wholeheartedly agreed to go to dinner with him. Three months later we were living with each other. I was only 19 years old when we moved in together and Tommy was 27.

Tommy had just quit a job that he had held with Sysco since he was 16 years old. He was going through a divorce from his first wife of 10 years and he was somewhat of a mess, personally and professionally. I looked past all of that because I liked him so much. We both had apartments, but I didn't want to move into his condo. My apartment had an extra bedroom, so he moved into my place. I just couldn't give up my own security. I didn't tell him that, but maybe he knew.

We lived in my apartment for one year. The first six months were turbulent but we were happy. Tommy called me his "little miss" and I felt like a princess much of the time. He waited on me hand and foot. I remember I had these slippers with big duck heads on them, which he hated. I would wear them to the grocery store and he never said a word about it. He let me be myself. His sister worked as a hair stylist and talked me into taking some cosmetology classes. While I was with Tommy, I completed all but the last 50 hours of the coursework, then quit. Maybe I was afraid of how a career would change my life. Maybe I was petrified of any change. Maybe I needed to be taken care of. Or maybe I was just a mess.

Not long into our relationship I began to think Tommy was selling drugs. He would take phone calls and step away so I couldn't hear the conversation. I had quit doing all drugs at this point so I didn't want to have anything to do with anyone who took them or sold them. He kept that part of his life separate from our shared life because he knew of my aversion to drugs. For a while, burying my head in the sand actually worked. I got good at pretending that we were fine; that he was not selling and using drugs on a regular basis. But I knew, deep down in my soul, what he was doing. I remember one night when we were out to dinner, he kept getting phone calls. I found out later he was dealing cocaine and marijuana. This event popped the bubble of my ignorance and all at once I had a strong gut feeling that I was going to get pulled into something very wrong.

Against my better judgment, I ignored the warning signs to leave.

We had lived together for several months before Tommy's brother-in-law from his previous marriage, Eugene came to stay with us. We fixed up the spare bedroom and he moved in. I think that is when Tommy started smoking crack cocaine because he became increasingly paranoid. He was extremely gaunt and his eyes, once my favorite feature of his, were sunken and almost devoid of feeling.

Eugene's girlfriend Joyce was over all of the time. I started noticing spoons in the sink, all bent up and black on the bottom. I asked Joyce about this and she said she didn't know anything about it. After that, she always wanted to do the dishes.

Tommy knew I hated the smell of pot, so he would only smoke in the back room; he, Eugene, and Joyce were always hanging out there. I never went back there. As before, I refused to see the truth.

One night things came to a head. Tommy was ignoring me and I was furious because he never ignored me. The living room was full of smoke and smelled like burnt rubber and pickles. It is a smell that you never forget. I went in the back room and saw Tommy smoking out of a crack pipe. I was horrified, disgusted, and confused all at the same time. And I went crazy. I got a knife and went after Joyce. Eugene tried to stop me but he was a very small guy. Tommy took my ID and burned it in the sink. It was a screamfest. Eventually one of the neighbors must have called the police. They came and when they asked me for my ID, I just pointed to the sink.

My thoughts focused on one thing, "Do I stay or do I go?" I felt trapped in a love that I knew was wrong but I could not break free. I had nowhere to go.

But I have had nowhere to go before. This time seemed different somehow. I just couldn't bring myself to be on my own, without him. Tommy promised he would change so I chose to stay. This was the first of many police visits which never resulted in me pressing any charges. I was afraid of being without Tommy so I never wanted to jeopardize our relationship. As dysfunctional as it was, it was all I thought I had.

Vacation

After about six months, Tommy got a job as an over-the-road truck driver. Before he started working full-time, we decided to go visit my mom in Florida. We brought a mutual friend Rebecca. She was not good. I knew her from a group home where we were constantly in trouble together. I assumed she had changed; grown up since we got out. But that was not the case. She was into prostitution and drugs. When we went on the trip to Florida, Rebecca was pregnant.

The trip set out to be smooth. I remember we were excited to be on vacation. Tommy brought $10,000 so we could have an extra-good time and not worry about money. The positive excitement soon turned into drama when we drove through New Jersey. Tommy was speeding and a police car turned on its siren to direct him to pull over. Instead, he got in a high-speed race with the officer. Miraculously, we got away.

Tommy knew a lot about cars and his car was fast. It came in handy for him that time, but as we approached the last exit before entering Florida, his luck ran out. A different policeman tried to pull him over. Tommy sped away, and as he did, his clutch blew. He went to get off at the exit and the police officer followed him, pulled him over, and pulled out his gun. Tommy was taken to jail. They towed and impounded the car. I was really scared because I knew he had crack pipes in the car but somehow they did not find them. Again, the luck of Tommy prevailed.

The crazy thing about this story is that the police officers at the jail gave Tommy a verbal court date for December and took $4,500 of his cash for "bail." Later, when we looked up the court date, we realized it was a Sunday. There was never a record of him being arrested and he never went to court. They just took the money.

We got the car out of impoundment and finally made it to my mom's apartment. Once there, Tommy would take me to "explore Florida," but he just wanted to buy drugs when we were driving around. The areas were not safe at times and at one point our car got swarmed with people wanting to sell him drugs. I was extremely nervous, but as always, Tommy got us out of the situation. I had a delusional, false sense of security that he could get us out of anything. At the time, what I didn't see was that Tommy always got us into trouble in the first place.

We went to the Guavaween Festival in Ybor on Halloween. This is one good memory I have of Florida.

During this festival, the city literally shuts down to car traffic and everyone walks around dressed up in really elaborate costumes. It was so much fun to gaze at all of the people, and the city was alive with excitement. While we were in Ybor, we decided to get a tattoo together. We both got a Chinese symbol for "faithful" on the same place on each of our necks. Other than that, most of the trip consisted of Tommy in a room with Rebecca smoking crack.

When we got home, the situation with Rebecca got progressively worse. She would meet guys online and hook up with them. After having sex, she would rob them at knifepoint. She then told her unsuspecting victims that she would lie and say they raped her if they tried to report her. Rebecca said if I didn't help her pull off this scheme, she would tell Tommy that I was involved and doing the same thing. For some reason, she was constantly trying to get me in trouble with him. I was afraid that she was out of control and I decided to confide in Tommy's sister about the extortion that Rebecca was threatening.

Unfortunately, she never believed the things I told her and she went to Tommy with the whole story. He got very mad and confronted Rebecca. She tried to fight me and I remember Tommy yelling for me to run. I hid in a hallway as they got into a screaming match. This ended the relationship with Rebecca. I couldn't help but feel bad because I didn't have any other friends. Again, it wasn't a functional friendship, but I was very secluded and with Rebecca gone, I felt more and more alone. I read online years later that Rebecca was serving time in jail because she stabbed her ex-boyfriend. I guess she had decided to still not grow up.

Around this time, we moved and my mom sent my sister Trisha up from Florida. Apparently Tricia was getting into trouble with drugs and with boys and my mom couldn't handle her anymore. I readily agreed for her to move in with us. It didn't take me long to figure out that my mom wasn't exaggerating about her behavior. I don't think I was very successful. One small example was her gothic appearance. When she would leave the house in a bra with nothing but a fishnet shirt over it, I would make her change her outfit. Soon, she started putting shirts she wanted to wear in the landlord's mailbox downstairs and changing on her way out the door. I know this because the landlord asked me why we were keeping our shirts in her mailbox.

I was gone a great deal of the time and I had big problems of my own. Even so, I had every intention of getting full custody of Trisha and I truly wanted to give her a home. I got the paperwork together, but Trisha kept hiding the forms. She wanted to live with me but she didn't want me to gain custody of her. Thinking back, she may have felt that I was trying to control her. Thinking back, I probably was.

On the Road

One good thing about being a dancer is that you can pretty much come and go as you please. Clubs always want dancers and your schedule is your own. If you want to work on a particular night, you come in. The more dancers they have, the more money they make. This "professional freedom" afforded me the "luxury" of riding with Tommy in the truck. There was a television and a DVD player in the cab. We went all over together. Sometimes I liked it but now I think I may not have known any better. It just was.

I passed some of the time on lengthy trips by falling in love with a puppy I bought at a truck stop in Texas. I named her Misery because she was so miserable when I bought her. She was literally starving and had a horrific flea problem. She would hide all the time because she was so afraid of everything and everyone. I loved that dog, but it wasn't long before Tommy got really mad because she was not potty-trained and she had constant accidents in the truck. He left her at a truck stop. It was a long time before I stopped crying.

After incidents like that, Tommy would do something nice for me and I would be right back in this obsessive need for him. One time, I had a terrible ear infection and he drove so fast to find a CVS that he brought down a power line. To me, that was twisted affirmation that he really cared for me.

I obsessively worried about getting pregnant. I had a large book in which I wrote every time we had sex in order to track my cycle. We were over the road in Texas when I took a urine test and found it was positive. I bought and took four more tests because I just couldn't believe it. That was the last time I wrote in the book.

I was terror-stricken. I had no idea how to be a mom and I knew Tommy was not in a place in his life to be a parent. By this time, Tommy was cheating constantly. I caught him once just by answering his phone and talking to his girlfriend. When I confronted Tommy, he swore it was a one-time thing. I'm pretty sure when I went into labor he was with that same girl.

I was a high-risk pregnancy because there was too much fluid in the amniotic sack, so I was on bedrest much of the time. Sometimes I would just lie in the back of the truck, but if I had a doctor appointment, I had to stay in the apartment. That being said, we had no car so I walked to my appointments. Toward the end of my pregnancy, I had to stay home all of the time. My downstairs landlord was an old Portuguese woman who fed me often and was very kind to me.

When I was eight months pregnant, Trisha did not come home at her curfew one night. I was worried and went out in the neighborhood searching everywhere for her. She came walking down the road with her pants unzipped and hanging half off of her body. I knew something very bad had happened to her. I forced her to walk to the hospital with me. Although I knew she needed one, she refused a rape kit. Trisha was out of control. I guess we both were.

A week later, a friend of mine gave me a baby shower. My mom came from Florida. No gift, but at least she came. I did get gifts from other people and it was a really wonderful day. The very next day I went into labor almost three weeks early. I was on the floor in such pain. I thought something was wrong. My mom was still there visiting; she rubbed my back and called the landlord to see what she should do. Of course, my dear old landlord recommended that she call an ambulance. Good advice! When I arrived at the hospital, they discovered that the baby was breech and they very quickly delivered a baby girl to me by caesarean section. Trisha went back to Florida with my mom and I went home with my daughter, August.

Tommy was gone all of the time and I was scared and lonely. I remember locking myself in the bathroom a few times when the baby cried. I just didn't know what to do so much of the time. Tommy was sure I had postpartum depression and insisted that I go to the crisis center. We asked his aunt to watch August and I was admitted into the hospital when she was only a few months old. Tommy went back on the road but he did try to call me several times. They had me on so many heavy drugs that I either could not answer the phone or could not talk if I was able to answer. I was only in the hospital for a few days before Tommy signed me out.

We decided that I would go back to school and Tommy's aunt would care for the baby during the day. So for several months, I would go to school, then go over to his aunt's house to be with the baby until it was time to go to bed. Then I would go home and do it all again the next day. After a few months, I felt ready to handle school and my daughter, so I made arrangements to bring August home. Tommy's aunt had different ideas; she outright refused to give August up. She accused me of not being fit and not being ready, but I just got the baby and left. Later, she told me she had burned the baby book I made for August. All of her baby memorabilia was gone.

When I got home, nothing had changed. Tommy was often gone and we were dirt-poor. Even when Tommy was home, he was completely and unreasonably paranoid. On top of that, it was very cold and I was even more isolated. I would bundle up the baby and take her for a walk just to get out of the apartment.

One memory I have in this dark time is of Tommy coming home, out of his mind. For some reason he said that someone outside on the street had told him that I had sex with someone. He was screaming and throwing things around the apartment, swearing that I was having an affair. He accused me of having the fictitious man's phone number, so he went through everything in the apartment looking for a piece of paper. He tore the heads off all of August's dolls and stuffed animals while looking for the paper. Even then, it wasn't until I saw that Tommy had a knife in his hand that I called the police.

As I picked up the phone to dial, he ripped the phone cord out of the wall. I ran with the baby downstairs to my landlord's and called the police. Together, that saint of an old lady and I waited for the police while Tommy screamed threats of suicide. Those 10 minutes felt like a lifetime.

When the police finally arrived, they went upstairs, but could not find Tommy anywhere. They were getting ready to leave because they felt that they had looked everywhere in the entire townhouse. My landlord and I knew he had not left because we had heard him yelling upstairs right up until they arrived. There was no back exit. Only by going past her door could he have left, and we were there the entire time.

We went upstairs together to look one last time and I was so relieved when one of the officers heard a noise from the couch. They turned the couch over and found Tommy coiled between the wood planks on the bottom like a snake.

Once again, I did not press charges.

This was one of many incidents with Tommy, too many to count. When I finally knew I had to leave, it was because of an attempted suicide. He had threatened suicide before, but during one particular trip to Georgia, Tommy called his boss and told him he was done. His boss was scared and drove me all the way to Georgia. I stayed in the car while he checked out the truck. He called an ambulance and later told me the cab of the truck looked like a crime scene. I don't know how Tommy got out of being in the psych ward after that episode. He got 76 staples in his arms and then was released. Tommy always did get out of everything.

After this incident, I started talking to my grandma in Florida. I knew August and I needed to leave. I finally got the courage to tell Tommy that August and I were moving. Tommy got a trip to Florida and offered to drive us there. I fit all of our possessions into a garbage bag, put August on my back, and headed into that truck. I listened to him beg me to stay for 18 hours while he drove us south.

When we got to Florida, I tried to stay with Trisha, but her house was infested with roaches. Right away I got into a verbal match with one of Trisha's friends; Tommy stepped in and the boyfriend of Trisha's friend got involved. The fight was so loud that the police were called. Apparently the boyfriend was 17 so Tommy was arrested and later returned to Massachusetts.

I called my grandmother and we were able to stay with her. That was a blessing.

My grandmother cooked and we ate well. I began to gain some much-needed weight. I was not in a healthy state of mind; nonetheless I started to feel better, safer.

My grandmother helped me with August. I started dancing at Showgirls and my grandma's husband would drive me to work. They did not judge me when I dated people, yet I knew I needed to get my own place. I got an apartment not far from their house and I settled into Florida.

Winifred Grace and Ava McCarthy

A Poem - Tattoos

The feel of fifteen tiny needles piercing into your skin could never compare to the pain that I felt, deep within my soul.

Tattoos and body piercings were my release from my negative reality.

The constant vibrating rhythm from the gun,
the slow trickle of blood,
the harsh rubbing with a dry napkin across the freshly inked area.

It was all my way of letting go,
going into another world,
an escape;
 from all the men hounding me at the club,
   from my girlfriend nagging,
     from my own twisted thoughts of wanting to cut.

Tattoos were my time not to feel numb.

I realized early on that tattoos
gave me more of a relief
than cutting.

If people saw color instead of scars,
Maybe
they would be less likely to try to read into my past.

Maybe.

Chapter 6 – Body Modification

Most of my tattoos were done when I was in Florida, but not all of them. When I was 18 and had just started dancing, it wasn't long before I found a customer to pay for the first of many. I told him it was my birthday and that he should take me to get a tattoo. He willingly obliged. My initial thought was to get a set of hands holding a rosary on my lower back with the cross just above my rear end. Not very classy now that I think about it. The tattoo artist said that he was not good at hands, so I settled for a heart with a fire-haloed cross coming out of it. Right above it was my grandfather's name, Caravelli.

I liked his name above this tattoo. Up until he died he was the only man in my life I ever trusted. He was an alcoholic who became extremely carefree when he drank. He would often give me and my sister money, shaped into various origami rings, and wonder where his money had gone the next morning. He also loved to record himself with a tape recorder. I have a cassette of him talking and it is invaluable to me. When he passed away, I was in the group home and wasn't permitted to attend the funeral. That day was easily one of the saddest days of my life. It only seemed appropriate to get something in remembrance of him.

A week after I got my first tattoo, I got my eyebrow and tongue pierced. I had a few random piercings over the years but surprisingly enough I am a big baby when it comes to piercings. But not with tattoos. Tattooing slowly began to replace the urge to cut. I thought tattooing was a less obvious sign of much deeper scars. I expressed my inner turmoil with colorful artwork.

I got three additional tattoos in the year after my first one. The first is on my lower back. It is a tribal symbol with two little monkey-looking gnomes on either side. One is holding a flower and the other is pointing at his weird friend. I do not remember who I was with but I do remember going into the tattoo shop and feeling on top of the world. I had so much cash in my pocket and I could have gotten anything. I have no idea why I settled for a flash art piece.[13]

The second tattoo that year is above my pelvic area and says, "Italy's Finest." My then-girlfriend, Catherine, convinced me that it would be a good idea. We were at some kind of fair and there was someone

---

[13] Flash is referred to as art that is just hanging on the wall. Nothing custom or unique about it.

tattooing outside of a tent. I remember it being so beautiful outside and the guy asking me if I was sure I wanted this tattoo. I said, "Fuck it." Now that I have had a child it is stretched out and illegible. It may not have been such a good idea after all.

The third tattoo was on my chest. I wanted the tattoo to look like four bear prints. Instead, they looked like raccoon feet. This tattoo has haunted me since day one. The paws were skinny-looking with only three toes. Everyone who saw them had a comment or a critique. Years later I have happily covered them with a beautiful rose.

Many of the images I got early on represented good and evil. Sometimes I would get one because of someone I loved at the time. Unfortunately, at this low time of my life, so many of the tattoos meant nothing more than something to do at the time. For instance, a flower and butterfly on my right hip match the tattoo of a bartender from my work at the time. I don't even remember her name.

In contrast, a tattoo I got in the center of my back reads "Ti amo bellisima," meaning "I love you, beautiful" in Italian. I got this for my grandmother. Another one with deep meaning is on my right ankle, an infinity symbol that has always reminded me of my little girl because she is the only thing I could love forever.

My life, at this time, was a seemingly endless search for something that I was unable to find. The entourage of partners marching in and out of my personal circus was a clown's mask covering my total unacceptance of myself. My life became a merry-go-round of partners with tattoos as tokens to elaborately illustrate each broken dream.

Catherine

Catherine was devious, intriguing, and beautiful all at the same time, a deadly combination. She was blonde, usually not my type, but for some reason her straight-girl, cheerleader appearance appealed to me. She worked at Subway and I worked at Balloons, a bikini bar in Rhode Island right behind Cheaters. I hung out with her a bit while she was at work and soon my flirting paid off because we ended up dating each other.

I was coming home with a shit-ton of money from dancing, and Catherine began getting jealous. The hard truth was, I could make in twenty minutes what she made in two weeks. She asked me to get her an audition and I reluctantly agreed. It turned out my apprehension was warranted.

I knew Catherine was straight before she dated me. I was prepared for the possibility that she might question our relationship when she began to work at Balloons. What I was not prepared for was her total lack of discretion about her sexuality. She would constantly cheat on me with guys she met at the club. Some of them were guys she liked and some were for money. I told her I didn't want any sexually transmitted diseases and she had to pick me or them. She chose them.

I maliciously decided to let two of the guys know that she was messing with them both at the same time. Her blatant infidelity culminated in an ugly fight right outside of the club. As a result, I got fired. It turned out that Catherine was also "seeing" the manager. Since she was living with me on and off at the time, she had full access to my beautiful apartment. I had a bad feeling leaving work the night of the fight, so I asked a bouncer friend to follow me home. That was the only good thing that happened that day because a "friend" of hers was outside of my apartment waiting for me. He left when he saw the size of my escort.

I entered my apartment to find that all of my furniture had been stolen. I had leather couches, a very expensive radio system with subwoofers, and a brand-new kitchen table and chairs. She took what she wanted and she literally pissed all over the rest. She also took all of my clothes that she liked and proceeded to cut up whatever was left. I had nothing. My self-esteem was immediately squelched. I had just started to gather possessions, just started to feel a sense of pride in ownership, a feeling new to me. In an instant, everything I had worked so hard to earn was demolished by one crazy bitch.

Catherine and I never spoke again. I did take a flyer from the club Balloons and I put it in her parents' home mailbox. I am sure that they were not happy that their daughter was now on the cover of the flyer. At the time, I didn't care what harm I caused. I wanted to hurt her like she had hurt me. I had a long way to go until I learned to control my emotions or understand pride in myself.

From there I stayed with a random selection of people. I'm not sure of their names or why I stayed. I had yet to give up drugs at this point in my life and I was high on a regular basis. I consistently went to get tested for sexually transmitted diseases. One test revealed that

I had contracted chlamydia and I had to tell the last two men I had been with sexually. Luckily they were supportive and we all went to the clinic together. One shot in the ass and it all went away.

I moved back to Massachusetts shortly after this and stayed with a friend in New Bedford. He lived with his sister and mother and I just stayed on the couch. I started dancing at the Kings Inn while I lived there.

Tommy

As illustrated in the previous chapter, Tommy consumed my life. While I was with Tommy I got three tattoos. I have a Chinese symbol which means "faithful." I have my daughter's name in a butterfly's wing on my right shoulder; I got that while I was pregnant with her. Lastly, I got a set of eyes crying on the back of my neck. I get a lot of questions about this one because of a single tear coming from one eye. When people ask about the one tear, I tell them, "Because it was at a rough point in my life." That is somewhat true but more accurately, the one tear shows that I was not weak. To me it showed that I can cry, but that I would always have one eye dry so that no one could see how vulnerable I was so much of the time.

In 2007, Tommy dropped me off in Florida and I started getting numerous tattoos. Some had meaning and some were just random because I needed to get rid of the "numbness" that I felt most of the time. It was like I was awake but not alive. I was in an emotional coma for years, going through the motions of an existence that protected me from any pain.

Bloom Where Planted

When I got my first tattoo in Florida, I had no car so the first shop that showed up on Google was where I told the cab driver to head. It was $25 each way and the tattoo itself was $250. I got a set of sparrows, one on the back of each arm: a devil and an angel sparrow. While I was in the tattoo shop, I saw a drawing of a rosary entwined around a rose. I really liked it so the following week I got that very drawing on my left ankle. Unfortunately, the next week my foot started swelling so much that my flip-flop would not even fit on my foot. I went to the hospital and discovered that I had gotten cellulitis, a type of staph infection. I hobbled around on crutches for weeks.

Doreen

When I met Doreen, she was a soccer player. She had moved to Florida to go to college on a scholarship. At the time, August and I had moved into my grandmother's house and I was sleeping on her couch. While I was with Doreen, she went with me to a local tattoo parlor and I got a koi swimming down my leg with cherry blossoms. No particular reason for this, I just liked the design. I found out later that a downward swimming koi is bad luck. A koi swimming up is good luck. Wish I had known that then.

Coralline

My next relationship was with a woman named Coralline. She worked at a gay bar in Ybor. She was very rich and very snooty but we had fallen for each other and we really had fun. It didn't work out because her parents would never approve of their daughter dating someone like me, a dancer.

I got a rainbow lambda symbol on my right wrist while I was with Coralline. Some guy from the club paid for it. I was told that the Greek letter symbolized "shining light into the darkness of ignorance." That meant a lot to me at the time and, as it turned out, my life was an illustration of the light trying to shine through. For whatever reason, I refused to recognize that light and continued on my dark path.

<u>Shay</u>

After Coralline and I broke up, I dated Shay. I met her at Showgirls playing pool and she was a really nice person. In my opinion, she was transgender, she was just not ready to come out and say that, or maybe she didn't realize it yet. The entire time we dated, I never saw the sexual parts of her body. Maybe that had some correlation with the fact that I treated her so badly.

I do not know why, but I cheated on her often. One night I was with some girl. Although I really don't remember her name, I went and got a tattoo of a rose on my right upper arm with this girl after we were together. When I came home, Shay was mad. I remember her yelling, "You smell like sex." She left me shortly after that and I don't blame her at all.

Allie

Allie was not a good person and I don't know why I stayed with her for a year. She was very manipulative and she stole a great deal of money from me. I came to find out that she had been dating her ex-girlfriend the entire time she was dating me. One time she brought a girl home and slept with her at our house. I left her after that episode.

Strangely, sometime after I left Allie, her ex-girlfriend showed up at my grandmother's house wanting to fight me. After some conversation, I suggested to her, "Why fight when we can get a tattoo together and piss off our mutual ex?" Together, we got a set of rainbow stars tattooed on our left shoulders.

<u>Jamie</u>

When I met Jamie, I can honestly say I loved her. I worked at Showgirls and she worked at a retail store at the time. She was the nicest girl I had ever met up until then. We had so much in common and our daughters were the same age. We had mutual friends and did everything together. We both got a Japanese tattoo meaning "Love Conquers All" in the same place on our sides. We got the tattoos in a hot dog stand that had been converted into a tattoo shop. It was very hot and very dirty but I remember we lay on the table together, back to back, and it felt right.

Sadly, she had a bad problem with pills during the time we were together. It just wasn't meant to be. I got a set of stars tattooed on my neck with Jamie. I never finished the pattern, it hurt too much. When we broke up I got a tattoo that means "Heart Broken" in Japanese tattooed on my wrist.

Priscilla

I met Priscilla at Showgirls through one of her friends. I told her that I wanted to meet up with her after work so we went out to an all-night breakfast place called Clocks. I got off at 3 a.m. and we stayed there until 7 a.m. She had a big, beautiful smile and we liked each other right away. I lived with August and a roommate at the time. Priscilla lived with her mom and her stepdad. I was with her for five months before August and I moved in with her. I got a girl sitting on a vine tattooed on my left shoulder after that.

I lived with her for almost two years. She was wonderful with August and it wasn't long before we decided to have a commitment ceremony. I got a tattoo of a puzzle piece with a heart and the date of our ceremony in it. Priscilla got the puzzle piece that fits with mine with the same date in the same place.

Her mom was from Germany and spoke German. Her dad was from Italy. Priscilla called me "Pupa" all of the time, meaning "little doll" in Italian. I got "Pupa" tattooed on the back of my neck and her name tattooed on my ankle. She got my name on her stomach.

I came to find out that she had a horrible cheating issue. She would be gone for long periods of time and I wouldn't know where she was. She just stopped picking me up from work. Then she started hanging out with some girl and went on several trips with her. When I found that out it ended our relationship.

I was a mess at this time. Tommy took August with him for a while and eventually moved to Virginia. He was married and for some reason, I thought this would be the best for my daughter. I just figured anything had to be better than her staying with me.

Viola

I don't remember where I met Viola. We never lived together and I think our relationship was based on using her as a designated driver. I remember telling her she couldn't drink if I was drinking. Looking back, she may have been straight and I don't know why she stayed with me because I don't think I actually liked her. I think I just didn't want to be by myself. I soon got tired of being so mean to her.

Lexis

Lexis was the ex-girlfriend of the girl Priscilla dated while she was with me. I sought her out intentionally because I wanted to get back at Priscilla.

We got an apartment together and I stayed with Lexis for about a year. One night we got really drunk and there was a man in the bar tattooing. I got her initials tattooed on my ring finger. She got my initials too. We woke up the next day and both said, "What the hell happened?" I got an L inside a computer heart on my right forearm. She got my initial on her arm in the same place.

Unfortunately, Lexis also had a cheating problem. I would get home and there were other girls in our house. That being said, when I did leave her it wasn't over her infidelity. It was for a different reason altogether.

I developed a cyst on my ovary; it ruptured sending me to the hospital for two weeks. I was in such pain and Lexis never came to see me, not one time. After I was released from the hospital, I got a cupcake next to an ice cream cone tattooed on my left forearm because I knew it would piss off Lexis. I met her at a restaurant; she saw the recent tattoos and she snatched my glasses off my face. I couldn't see to drive home. When I finally got a ride home, we argued and she got physical with me. I was done with physical abuse in my life, hence I was done with Lexis.

After we broke up, I got a tattoo across my collarbone that says "Love equals Pain." I got the tattoo in the same bar and from the same artist who had tattooed Lexis's initials on me. I just lay down in the tattoo chair and let that artist do his thing.

Angie

Lexis moved out and I stayed in the apartment. I got a roommate whom I danced with but it turned out she was an escort. I didn't know this when she moved in because I never took her to work. She paid me to use my car so I did not know where she was going. One night, she was supposed to pick me up from work at Showgirls and I kept calling her but she would not pick up the phone. Eventually, I called the cops and told them my car was stolen by my roommate. I turned on the news the next day and learned she was involved in a big prostitution ring in Polk County. I saw my car being towed away on television. I had to get my car out of impoundment and Angie's face was plastered all over the news for prostitution on Craigslist. Needless to say, I lost yet another roommate.

By this point, I had started back at school. Unfortunately, if I wanted to transfer my credits from the previous school in Massachusetts, I would have to pay back my past student loans. I decided to start from the beginning of the program in the new school and pay cash rather than pay the past loans. This would not be the first time I would make a poor financial decision that would come back to haunt me.

Jackie

I met Jackie while working at Showgirls. She worked at Verizon. When I decided to approach her, Jackie was at Crabby Bills playing volleyball. We sat on the dock after a game and I told her that we should hang out. At first, she said she didn't know if she was interested. After the game broke up everyone snuck into the pool at the hotel next door. We swam in our underwear and had a really fun time. We started dating after that.

I ended up moving to Plant City, which was closer to work and to school. Jackie developed a problem with pills and I was done with that in my life so it didn't work out. Apparently, God had different plans in store for me.

Annie

I didn't know it at the time, but my life was about to change and I with it.

I met Annie at a bar in Ybor. I went to the bar with a girl who really liked me but when a mutual friend introduced me to Annie, I told my friend that I was going to marry her. Annie said, "Hi nice to meet you," and walked away. I told my friend to take the girl I was with to another bar and I spent the entire night searching for Annie. Just as I was about to give up, I saw her getting ready to leave the bar. I asked her, "Are you old enough to drink?" and she assured me that she was. She told me she was having a party at her house but I asked her to stay and we danced until the lights came on. When it was time to go, I made the girl I came with drive Annie home too. Annie put my number in her phone that night, twice.

Over the next several years, I got a crayon labeled with Annie's name on the inside of my arm, a sentence that reads, "I love you and I'll follow you anywhere," and flowers on my arms and chest, which I got with her. I have a tattoo of her lips on my hip.

Of all the tattoos I have gotten, the only ones that Annie asked me to change were Lexis's initials on my ring finger and Priscilla's name on my ankle. I got a rose tattooed on my ankle and Annie paid to have a bow placed over the tattoo on my ring finger. I wear my engagement ring over it. The tattoo on my ring finger is the only one I regret.

Chapter 7 – The Turning Point

Ever so slowly, my life started to change. When I met Annie, I was a dancer and a mom without custody of my daughter. Today I am a business owner, a student who is just a few classes away from being a college graduate, and the mother of a beautiful daughter who is happy, healthy, intelligent, and of good character. But as we know, the process of change is slow and it is hard.

Real change must come from first recognizing that there is, in fact, a problem; then, through planning and hard work, through fortitude and tenacity, through resilience and sheer will, change happens. It comes from pushing through hard lessons and constantly reaching for a better life. My change also came through forgiveness. Forgiveness for the good of those who harmed me, as well as for my own peace and well-being. And joy follows.

Unfortunately, these things do not always occur in our time frame. It seems as though there are prices that life charges for bad, past decisions.

This chapter is written from both my perspective and that of my partner. Looking back, it is a blessing how our intersection in this big world changed us both. We are individually better people because we were brought together.

Ava about Annie

When I first met Annie, she had just ended a serious relationship and was trying to find herself. She was doing anything and everything, trying to figure out her place in life. She was in therapy learning how to accept herself and others for who they are. What I saw was a girl who just needed to let go and have some fun.

Annie was dating four people when we met. Actually, a girl was supposed to move in with her at the end of the summer. When she told me about the girl, I said, "Oh, that's not a problem." The girl never moved in.

<u>Annie about Ava</u>

When I met Ava, I was convinced I would never sacrifice my happiness for anyone or anything ever again. Mix that mentality with Ava's "my way or the highway" mindset and it wasn't always pretty. Needless to say, we fought quite a bit. When we did fight, she would literally leave. It was not uncommon for her to say, "Okay, well fuck you, bye," and walk out.

Winifred Grace and Ava McCarthy

We met at a time in my life when I would never be manipulated again, and Ava was the queen of manipulation. I don't know why we stayed together. Possibly because Ava was the first person who really accepted me for myself. With Ava, I just came into my own and she never feared any part of me. She never judged me.

Even so, it was an unhealthy relationship for years.

Ava always kept the upper hand in any cards dealt to her. She is smart and she grew up wielding her intelligence toward survival. A huge portion of her energy went into her gaining control in any way possible. At first, I felt for her. She already had everything monetarily she needed, but she needed someone to believe in her: in her past, in her perseverance, in her goodness, and in her dreams. As I began to believe in her, I began to see her grow. I saw her changing.

When I met Ava she could not even go in elevators, so going on a plane was out of the question in her mind. She had never flown and was extremely claustrophobic because of being locked in bathrooms and closets much of her childhood. I said, "Well, this isn't going to work out then because my family lives in Ohio." She courageously bought a ticket to come home with me for my birthday. It was a tough first flight accompanied by a lot of tears. I held her hand the whole time and put a movie on the laptop. She pushed through, a big step for her.

I think I stayed in this relationship because I always knew Ava was good deep down. I kept asking her why she would do the things that she did, because it became more and more evident to me that she was intelligent, caring, thoughtful, and motherly. To me, her actions contradicted her true being. The person whom I felt so privileged to get to know just did not match up to the life she was choosing to live.

For instance, it seemed incomprehensible to me that Ava gave her daughter to Tommy. But the more we peeled away Ava's past, the more truth was exposed, the clearer the picture became.

She was told repeatedly throughout her life that she was a bad daughter, a bad partner, a bad human. In her heart, she truly believed it was better for August to be with Tommy. The way Ava saw it at the time, giving up August was the one gift she could give to her daughter.

I feel as though Ava and I grew up together. We found in each other a little bit of what each of us wanted to be. I needed to be more fun, carefree, take more risks, and live for now. Ava needed more stability, honesty, and dependability. She wanted normalcy. To get these two extremes together took time and more work than imaginable.

In the Beginning – Ava about Annie

Right after I met Annie, I sent flowers to her work. I had no idea that would turn out to be a big ordeal. How could I have known that she didn't want other people to find out she was serious with one person? I did not know that Annie would be embarrassed at work trying to explain who I was to her co-workers, or any of her other prospects. She didn't talk to me for weeks after the flowers. I thought for sure, "That's the end of that."

When she finally contacted me, she texted me when I was at a bar with another girl, my ex-girlfriend Priscilla, and her girlfriend. Annie simply stated, "I'm bored." Although I was eager to respond to her text, I had already had a few too many drinks. I called her the next day and we made plans to attend a big gay/lesbian event in Orlando. I was excited that she agreed to go with me but unaware of her intentions of checking out other women at the event. She was definitely not in a place where she wanted a serious girlfriend. I think I was more like a sociology project to her.

We had a great day and, afterward, we went to Chili's. As we sat in the booth, I turned my head and saw a yellow dove sitting outside the window. Strange, a yellow dove just sitting there looking at us. I think about it still.

I was dancing at Showgirls at this time and once in a while Annie would come to the club, but she never saw me dance. When she visited, all the dancers would come to talk to her because they thought she had such a cute body. At this time, I knew I wanted to do hair, but for some reason I just could not leave the club. I made so much money and it made me feel wanted; more than wanted, it made me feel needed. I called the club "The Black Hole" and told Annie, "No one gets out." The twisted fame and perverse attention suck you back in every time you try to leave.

When I met Annie, I lived in a two-bedroom apartment in Plant City. Even though I did not have custody of August, I wanted her to have a place to stay when she visited.

It didn't take long before I was staying at Annie's house on a pretty regular basis. We could not get enough of each other. I had a space in her closet and it made me happy. She called me "stripper girl." We were together all of the time, but it was a tumultuous relationship.

Annie and I began to have long conversations about what I wanted to do, who I envisioned myself to be, personally and professionally. I finished hair school and within the first few weeks of starting to date Annie, I slowly began to try my hand at cutting hair. Although I had tried to get August so many times over the years, we began to talk about custody in such a way that I seriously started to imagine it might happen. For the first time, I had hope. That being said, I had no clue how to be in a "normal" relationship and it got me in trouble multiple times.

Not long into our relationship Annie went home to Ohio for a wedding. She invited a friend from home to attend with her. I just really did not understand why she would go with another girl. I had no point of reference because I had never been to a wedding in my life. I had no idea how to trust that she could date me and go to this wedding with a friend.

While she was in Ohio, a mutual friend asked me to go to a party at Annie's ex-girlfriend's house. Annie asked me not to go, but at the time, getting back at her for leaving me and going to that wedding was of more interest to me.

Winifred Grace and Ava McCarthy

At first, everyone at the party was having fun, playing beer pong and talking. Unfortunately, things turned sour as the night progressed. As it would happen, I somehow ended up in a room with Annie's ex. We just talked, but the conversation was negative and targeted at Annie's character. Her ex-girlfriend talked about why I shouldn't date Annie. "She is controlling. She will try to control you. She will leave you in the end." I got out of the room and left the party but it caused damage to our young relationship.

This incident was the first of many times when issues from my past would get in the way of having a functional relationship. It took me a very long time to begin to understand trust. I struggle with it still. Sometimes I have to remind myself that I am good enough to be in a real relationship.

In the Beginning– Annie about Ava

The night of the party, I called her and asked if my ex was going to be at the party and, of course, she lied. I was in a mall in Ohio with a friend when Ava told me she went to that party. My heart broke and I just cried.

This new relationship had escaped my very toxic history. That night, I felt as if the dark cloud of my stormy past had blown into my present. I was devastated. Eventually I forgave her, but it took a long time and a much deeper understanding of just how dark Ava's history had been. Her wounds ran deeper than most and they were covered up with years of survival instincts central to her very nature.

Winifred Grace and Ava McCarthy

The first year of our relationship, Ava had fits constantly. She would scream and cry, completely shut down both physically and mentally.

We would break up and I would call other people. I would say "forget it" and hang out with another girl. I would tell myself that Ava was expendable. But then in the morning, I always wanted Ava. We were young and immature and both in bad places. I would do a bad thing and she would do a bad thing and then we would forgive each other. Looking back, if I had to classify this relationship I would say it was dysfunctional and beyond repair.

Many times during the rocky start of our relationship, I thought, *I have to get out of here.* That same thought and countless others crossed my mind multiple times the entire first year we were together.

Why am I doing this? This is not right. She will never change. She will always be like this. But the problem was, I kept wanting to be with her.

There was something else. In the beginning, I was embarrassed that I was with her. Usually after a fight, from the darkness there would be intermittent little beams of hope that poked through. I could see that Ava was, and is, the most accepting person I have ever met. She accepted me wholeheartedly. She accepts everyone for exactly who they are, no judgment. Nonetheless, even with the flickers of hope, I knew she would need more than me to help her see light.

Six months after we met, Ava knew she had to seek custody of August. She started to see that something was very wrong with Tommy. He had met and married a woman named Deedee and August began to share very bizarre stories about her stepmom. It became very clear that August was no longer safe with Tommy. It was then that Ava began the long, arduous battle to regain custody of her daughter.

When I saw Ava take charge and try to get August back, I started to be seriously interested in her. Seeing her fight so hard to do what was right, and make so many changes in the first year of our relationship, made me want to be with her even more. I kept seeing more and more of who she really was and I saw all that she could be. I believed in her. And, I think, she believed in me. I began to commit to her but I knew she needed help. And I knew who could help her.

The Right Therapist – Annie

Bloom Where Planted

I had started seeing Troy about a year before I met Ava. After my last break-up, I was a mess. I knew I didn't want to be the kind of person I was becoming. I knew I was in a cycle and I had to break out of it. Troy helped me do that.

When I met Ava, I was growing healthy and in the process of changing. We had the same view on mental health, that ultimately she was in control of her moods, her thoughts, and her actions. She, of all people, knew that she had the power to overcome adversity, negativity, and old cycles.

Very early in our relationship I suggested that Ava see Troy. I knew in my heart he could help her. It took her almost a year to start seeing him and she walked out in the middle of her therapy sessions almost as many times as she went. I bet Troy wishes he had a dime for each time Ava said her famous line, "Okay, well fuck you, bye." But she always went back. It was Ava who had to make the choice to keep returning to therapy.

Troy is different than most therapists. He would accept nothing less than change. In my experience with Troy, he has never been wrong in his advice but it comes out so crass, it can be offending upon initial impact.

One time he told Ava and I, "It is not easy to be with a survivor." For some reason, this short statement helped me to understand Ava more completely. For years and years, it was in Ava's very core to survive at all cost. She never let her guard down. She was like an animal always looking for the predator that she knew was lurking, just waiting to pounce.

Everything for Ava was in the present. Never, ever was there a thought for anything beyond surviving the day. When she danced, it was not uncommon for her to make $800 in a day and then not work for the rest of the week. Living only in the temporary, never trusting to look beyond right now. It was exhausting to be with someone who just survived.

Troy taught us how to disagree in a productive way. I always think I am right. Ava is a survivor. Her thought was, "I will get you before you get me." My thought was, "Do whatever you want because I am right and you will see that in the end." It was a very volatile combination. What Troy taught us was quite simple: "Do you want to fight or do you want to solve the problem?" When we finally got together on that simple question, the relationship became the priority.

I remember one exercise consisted of us standing together facing each other; I would say, "I'm right," and

Ava would say, "I love you, I'll follow you anywhere." That is exiting the fight. We had to learn that the relationship was more important than being right. We had to know that we were united. We had to know that where one of us would go, no matter the direction, the other would follow. We had to know that this person was who each of us wanted to be with and worth fighting for, not against.

Not long after that session, we went to a tattoo parlor and I wrote "I love you, I'll follow you anywhere" on Ava's arm. They traced my handwriting with a tattoo gun and we added Troy's initials after the quote.

The Right Therapist – Ava

When I first started seeing Troy I could not stand him. Actually, I hated him. For a long time, I refused to listen to what he was saying and outright rejected working on any of his suggestions. I constantly would leave his office in the middle of a session screaming, "Fuck you." If, for any reason, I would complain about anything in my relationship with Annie, he would just say, "Then break up."

Sometimes I would quit going for a while after one of my fits. Other times I would call from the parking deck and ask if I could come back. He would always let me come back, even the same day.

Even though he said things I did not like to hear, somewhere along the rough road to recovery, I started to like him. From the very beginning, I knew that he cared about me. When I gave him grief, he would not engage with me. Never, ever did he sugarcoat anything. It was always exactly as he saw it whether you liked it or not.

Troy always held me accountable. I thought that was respectful. He respected himself and he respected me. He cared enough to back me down, to say the exact truth without confusion or a hidden agenda. He showed me compassion, respect, and love. He treated me like a human being.

I went twice a week for a year and then once a week for years. I still see him and, quite honestly, I don't know if I would have been as successful at changing my life without his help.

The Move – Annie

When I got accepted at the University of Central Florida, I asked Ava to come with me to Orlando. I was 23, headstrong, and decided to become engaged. At the time, same-sex marriage was not legal, so we did not move forward with a wedding. Thinking back, I am glad we didn't. We were two totally different people. We were together, but I think of how we are now compared to how we were then; we were together but not in a completely functional way. When you go through hardship with someone, you really know that person. It pushes you together.

The bikini bar Ava had worked at for six years was too far from Orlando for her to commute so she couldn't fall back on dancing. She was forced to find a different professional path. She began cutting hair as a career and quit three separate salons in a short amount of time. Well actually, she quit two and got fired from one.

Once she was hired at Hair Cuttery, she settled down. She was quickly promoted to Assistant Manager and we were happy, she was learning. She did great and

I was proud of her. But looming, always just beyond our reach, was August.

The Move-Ava

Annie had been unhappy at her job, so she decided to make a career move and applied to a master's program in Orlando to study Marriage, Couples, and Family Therapy. When we got the call announcing that Annie had been accepted into the program, we immediately packed and moved to Orlando. We got an apartment together and decorated a room in Hello Kitty patterns for August. Even though we did not have her, I couldn't wait to show her. I thought about her all the time.

I didn't have trouble finding jobs when we moved, I had trouble keeping jobs. Someone would do something wrong and I would leave. I had no tolerance for anything that I thought was stupid. When I finally found Hair Cuttery, I felt like I settled down. I began to sell merchandise and was top salesperson multiple times. I won competitions and it wasn't long before I was promoted to Assistant Manager. Little by little, there were glimpses of hope.

I took a leap of faith, stopped dancing, and began working solely at cutting hair. The money difference between dancing and making a regular wage as a new hair stylist in a new location with no regular clients was a vast cutback. I had no idea how to budget, how to pay back past debt, or even what a credit score was. What I had done in my financial past had caught up with me at a time when I was making the least amount of money. It was difficult. For years it seemed like I would take a step forward and two steps back much of the time. I just kept moving forward and trying harder.

Getting August Back - Ava

Every spare cent we had went into getting August back, including Annie's loan money for school. It was not easy or cheap, but we were determined and united in our cause. It seemed like every time a road block entered our path, a side-road opened.

When I began the process, we still lived in Tampa. As soon as I started to see signs that August was not doing well with Tommy, I knew I had to get her back. The first thing I did was sell all the jewelry I owned to pay for a plane ticket to Virginia. It hurt my pocket, but the flight hurt me so much more. It was excruciating for me to be in small, confined areas. It took a great deal of effort for me to push through the fear.

My first court experience could be described as a travesty of justice. I had no money for a lawyer and the guardian ad litem was very much against my lifestyle. Tommy and his wife told so many outright lies about my past that falsehoods were published about me in the finalized court documents. It was a very dark time for me.

After we moved to Orlando, we were granted a second court appearance and we hired a lawyer in order to take the necessary steps to get joint custody with set visitation. The end goal: to gain full custody of August. Unfortunately, the lawyer was young and inexperienced in court and did not serve us well in our cause. One time, we drove up to Virginia to find that Tommy and his wife had not even shown up in court. We had to reschedule, turn around, and drive home. Also, I had been paying child support in cash directly to Tommy and it was not in the court records. Therefore, I had to pay all back child support in order to gain visitation rights.

Annie and I would fly or drive to Virginia on a regular basis to get August for visitation. Eventually, the time came to pursue full custody. I dropped the inexperienced lawyer and obtained a phenomenal one. So began a nearly yearlong custody battle. We had to drive 12 hours every time we had court hearings. We would leave after Annie was done with work; drive through the night, then sleep at a hotel for three or four hours; wake up and go to court.

There were so many hoops to jump through. We went through the court process four times before we finally made headway. I remember one time we drove all the way to Virginia just to have the court date postponed. It was a terrible time in our lives, but we knew that August would be better with us as she was experiencing problems in many areas of her young life.

One time before we had to take her back to Tommy's, she looked at me with tears in her eyes and said, "What are we going to do Mommy. How will we get back together?" There were times I couldn't go see her because we were paying so much to the lawyer and child support that we couldn't afford the visit. This broke my heart. Again, I had created a situation and it was more painful than I can say to go through the slow process of repairing a life that was broken.

Getting August Back – Annie

August's health was questionable to say the least. She was sick all of the time and her teeth were a mess. She had an overbite and rotting teeth. We had one tooth pulled almost immediately when we got visitation because it was hurting her so badly and when we had it checked, the dentist said it was literally broken off in her mouth. We had a second tooth pulled shortly thereafter.

During one visit we were told she would have to have spacers because one of the larger back teeth that had been pulled would cause all of her teeth to grow in crooked. Tommy and Deedee outright refused to get any dental work done, so August's teeth continued to deteriorate. We did the best we could when we had her with us.

August, however, did not exactly help with the oral hygiene problem. She did great brushing her teeth when she was with us. She absolutely refused to do so when she was with them, possibly her way of taking control the only way she knew how. When we would get her for visitation, there would be dirt caked on her head and behind her ears. It was quite possibly the most horrible time of our lives, to know she was getting worse and we couldn't help her right then, when she needed it the most.

In school, August's grades were terrible and her attendance was horrific. She couldn't read. When we asked Tommy and Deedee to get her tutored, they refused. When we offered to pay for tutoring, they opted to hold her back in first grade instead. She had such a lisp and could not pronounce her r's so you could barely understand her speech. We offered to pay for speech therapy, but again, they refused.

Winifred Grace and Ava McCarthy

I have learned that if you concentrate on what you can control, find the good that is in your power, any bad will surface on its own. In other words, you don't have to help bad along.

Around Christmas time, Tommy came to pick up August after a visit to my mom's in Ohio. Ava saw burn marks on his thumb. He did a good job of trying to hide his hands in his pockets, but Ava knew the signs. He was smoking crack again.

In February, we found out August had missed 38 days of school. Tommy and Deedee only allowed August to call us via speakerphone. As we talked to her, we could hear Tommy's wife turning August against us with lies. We had no chance to repair the relationship or try to calm August's worries with Deedee monitoring the conversations.

Bloom Where Planted

It was not long before we got the feeling that something else was up. One day, Deedee called us and said they were on a Greyhound and moving. She had pulled August out of school. Deedee told us that rats were living in their house and their droppings were making August sick. The phone monitoring made sense then. She did not want August to say anything about the rats or the move. We called the inexperienced lawyer and he said there was nothing we could do. That very day we hired our new lawyer. You could tell right away that he was on top of things and that he believed in Ava. The timing couldn't have been better.

Finally, our day in court came. We still believe that August's first-grade teacher in Virginia was an angel. She loved August so very much and she agreed to be a witness for Ava and me. August rarely bathed, rarely went to school, rarely did any homework, and was failing first grade for a second time. She was a little girl in trouble.

A terrible custody battle took place over the next year. Thankfully, we had a strong lawyer, a fantastic guardian ad litem, and God's guiding presence. (We still send our lawyer Christmas cards each year.) It took a very long time but good prevailed. Along with kindness, honesty, intelligence, a lot of money, and prayer. We prayed nonstop; screaming prayers, crying prayers, pleading prayers, and ultimately begging prayers.

We got August back with no clothes, no toys, no books, nothing. We went from court to Target, Toys "R" Us, Barnes and Noble, and Justice.

Unfortunately, Tommy and Deedee had told August many, many lies about Ava not wanting her and that she would be back with them by the end of the summer. August was angry and confused. She was sad about not seeing her dad and she missed her dog.

But time, beautiful time, heals all wounds.

It wasn't long before Tommy's marriage dissolved and, sadly, he has been incarcerated twice since we gained full custody.

The cycle had to be broken. We immediately put August in speech therapy and reading tutoring, twice a week, through the summer. Once she entered second grade, she had speech therapy in school and tutoring after school for a year. August focused her attention on math, on reading, and on speech. Together, we worked diligently after school and over weekends on sight words and flash cards. We hung words all over her bedroom walls and we played word games constantly. If she didn't have homework, we used workbooks to supplement her after-school learning.

Thankfully her second-grade teacher was an outstanding educator and human being. We really do not think August would have made the progress she did that first year if we had not had that perfect teacher. She loved August and we loved her.

I graduated with my master's and we decided to raise August in Tampa. By the time we were ready to move, we resembled a functional family.

I believe everything happens because of God's involvement. There were also catalysts in our recovery story. For instance, when we moved to Orlando, Ava stopped dancing, and she got her first good job. We were able to get August, and she got us. I got the experience I needed to have my current career.

Bloom Where Planted

We did not like living in Orlando; most of our memories from that time are negative, but now it seems so clear, "To everything there is a season and a time to every purpose under heaven." (Ecclesiastes 3:1)

We have worked very hard to become functional. I needed a survivor and Ava needed an anchor. And August needed both of us. We continue to see Troy when we need to, we go to church, we have stable careers, we value and respect each other, and together we are moving forward in love.

Epilogue

Mine is a story of an abused, oftentimes discarded person who chose to change and find the necessary support to do so. I have worked very hard to break the cycle of my past. I do not know why it took someone in my family so long to break free. I do not know why it was me who finally stopped the vortex but I thank God for the chance to recover and for being with me every step of the way. He was a silent warrior on my unknowing and oftentimes unwilling behalf.

If you are reading this book and are an abuser, have been abused, or are currently being abused, help is out there and change is within your grasp. Seek change. There is hope within every circumstance.

If you are reading this book and have not known abuse, try to understand that there are many people who have lived through very traumatic experiences. My hope is that you seek to judge less, feel more, and always be more accepting of difference.

We hope that you gain some perspective of the life of survival that many of our children in the United States are forced to experience because of broken homes. We do not mean to say that all foster experiences are the same, but only that this was the experience of one child who was lost in the system. Here is to hoping that we do a better job of seeing abuse, recognizing that there is a problem, and ultimately doing something about it. We can do this by taking action on several different levels:

1. Becoming a foster family to a child in need of a loving home. According to the U.S. Department of Health and Human Services and the Administration for Children and Families (https://www.afc.hhs.gov/cb, 2017), there were

437,465 children reported in the foster care system as of September 30, 2016.
2. Writing or calling politicians to voice your opinion on the public health care system in the United States.
   a. Higher pay level for those in the public health profession.
   b. Lower foster children-to-case worker ratios so that these dedicated warriors can spend more quality time with each child, thus lowering fatigue and burn-out in this stressful profession.
3. Reporting and following up on suspected incidents of child neglect and abuse.

It takes a joint effort to raise children in this great nation. We have the right, the obligation, and the responsibility to protect and serve ALL children. It's time we started doing just that.

Made in the USA
Middletown, DE
27 October 2018